D1587775

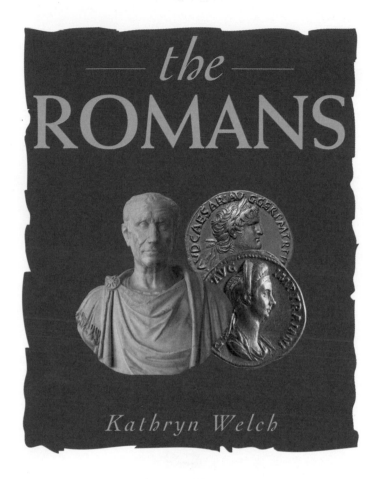

the ROMANS

Kathryn Welch

With Estelle Lazer
and
Jonathan Barlow

LANSDOWNE

937
1293081

Contents

Introduction 6

1. Vines, Pastures and Olives — a Pact with the Gods 8

2. "I am a citizen of Rome" 22

3. "I came, I saw, I conquered" 36

4. The Women of Ancient Rome 48

5. Perils of City Life 64

6. High Society on the Bay of Naples 80

7. Roman Emperors — Divine Rulers or Mad? 80

8. Games, Gladiators and Circuses 98

9. The Carrot and the Stick — a Slave's Life 110

10. Death and the Afterlife 121

11. The Coming of Christianity 133

12. The End of Empire 144

Some Important Dates in Roman History 150
Further Reading 155
Index 158

INTRODUCTION

"The Romans" means many different things and this work only introduces the reader to some of them: the people of the city state who bit by bit brought all Italy and then the Mediterranean under their control; the leaders who commanded armies and governments; the great figures of literature who consciously raised the level of the Latin language to the point where it could compete with the great literature of Greece; the emperors, most famous now, as then, for the ways they tried to wield absolute power; the subjects who lived in an empire which stretched from the ends of Spain and much of Britain across to Asia Minor and the Levant and down to Egypt and North Africa; the culture which changed the face of Europe and laid the foundations of Western Civilisation.

Rome was founded sometime in the eighth century before Christ. By 146 BC the Republican city state controlled the Mediterranean. Under its monarchy, founded in 28 BC, it led an empire until the fifth century of our era. The legacy of "Romanisation" meant that in some senses the Roman Empire did not really fall, although the city itself lost its power. The Empire in the East continued until the Fall of Constantinople in 1453 and kings in Medieval and Renaissance Europe styled themselves "Holy Roman Emperors".

6

This book looks at the men and women of Rome over its long history. It examines their myths, their religion, their governments, their entertainments, their army, the great men who formed the Empire and the emperors who ruled it. It traces some of the transformations which Rome and the Romans both caused and suffered. Above all, through this book, we experience the City, at its height a teeming metropolis of over a million people, which served as a magnet for all the peoples who had the means to travel to it. From the gleaming heights of the temples on the Capitol to the crowded tenements housing peoples of all origins, the city of Rome dominated the imaginations of observers as much as it ever controlled a world empire.

7

Vines, Pastures and Olives — a Pact with the Gods

Today, Rome is known as "the Eternal City". Everywhere the Romans conquered they encouraged and developed the growth of cities. Yet this greatest of ancient cities sprang from a pastoral beginning. Its ideals and legends were intimately associated with the Italian landscape. The legends of rustic Italy never died out even when sophisticated Romans built roads and bridges, carved their way through the forests, reclaimed the marshes and pushed the power and organisation of Rome to ever further limits.

The Beginning of Rome

The tiny settlement which became Imperial Rome was founded traditionally in the eighth century BC. According to legend, its founders were members of the neighbouring royal family of Alba Longa, a community of the Latin people who controlled much of central Italy. Nearby were the Sabine people, also Latins, who decided to join the Romans in founding their city rather than fight against them.

Early Rome lived in the shadow of the surrounding Etruscan nations whose civilisation produced a rich heritage of technology and luxurious living. For a time, Rome fell under Etruscan power and was ruled by Etruscan kings. These kings were eventually removed and a Republic instituted. The traditional date for this is 509 BC. Eventually Rome grew great enough to defeat and dominate its Etruscan neighbours.

▲ *Map of the Roman Empire in the time of Trajan (AD 98–117). The Empire ringed the Mediterranean from the time of Augustus (28 BC–AD 14) but Trajan added Dacia though it was soon lost. The eastern and southern desert borders are uncertain.*

▼ *This pastoral scene from a 3rd century AD sarcophagus from Rome depicts shepherds tending their sheep. The ideal of country life was an important part of Roman culture throughout its history.*

Rome Expands

Within two hundred years, Rome dominated the other peoples of Italy such as the mountain peoples. This was not an easy task. The fierce Samnites to the southeast very nearly defeated the Romans on many occasions. The Romans also conquered the Greek speaking peoples settled around the Bay of Naples, Campania, the foot of Italy and Eastern Sicily. Most of these cities had maintained a close relationship with the Greek city states which had founded them. Through this contact and an active interest in trade they provided Italy with a direct link to the civilisations of Greece and Asia Minor, present day Turkey. They had brought their gods with them, the gods of the woodlands as well as the gods of Olympus and the mythological stories surrounding them. Rome with its roots in native Italy stood in the middle of the traditions of Etruria and Greece, a crossroads of culture and ideas. Rome developed a religion that was a mixture of native Italian elements, Etruscan ritual and Greek mythology.

Guardian Spirits

Native Italian tradition saw the divine as a series of spirits without real personality. Each element within a thing or being was ruled by a guardian spirit. Most important were the household gods, the Lares, the spirits of the household, and the Penates, the gods of the cupboard who would see to the security of family prosperity. Each household had its guardian Lares as did each city and each state.

▶ *Shrine of the household gods (lararium) in the House of the Vettii in Pompeii. The Lares represented the spirits of place and acted as guardians of those who lived within their space. The snake represents the male generating spirit.*

◀ *Gold coin of Marcus Brutus produced c.43 BC after he had murdered Julius Caesar. He pictures either himself or an ancestor, ringed by the oak leaf crown, awarded to those who saved the lives of citizens.*

▶ *Stucco decoration from the ceiling of a house from Late Republican Rome. The scene shows an idyllic landscape including Priapus, an ancient fertility god, and idealised buildings, trees and general lushness.*

11

Nature was guarded by spirits. Trees and parts of trees, rivers and buildings each had a share of these spirits. Even the great drain of Rome, the Cloaca, had a guardian spirit, Cloacina. Humans had not just one guardian but a guardian for each separate bodily part. Specific to humans was their genius, the power to generate both the life of the individual and the formation of new life in a different generation. These guardians fostered prosperity in humans, animals and the land.

Etruscan Religious Influences

The Etruscans contributed the great Triad to the Roman religious scheme. Jupiter (also Jove), Juno and Minerva were the names given to the guardians of the Roman Capitol, the ancient citadel of legendary Rome. Etruscan learning also taught the Romans how to ascertain the will of the gods in specific circumstances. Officials called augurs used ritual to read the flight patterns of certain birds, animal intestines or other signs to know such important details as success in battle or whether an election had the approval of the gods.

▼ *Bronze model of a sheep liver from northern Italy. The liver of animals was an important tool for divining the will of the gods in Etruscan religion. Seers had to be taught how to read the signs or "auguries". Rome adopted Etruscan methods of divination and even sent some of its young men to Etruria to learn the sacred arts.*

▲ *Bacchus, the god of wine, is dressed in a bunch of grapes in front of Mt Vesuvius and its vineyards in this picture from a lararium in the House of the Centenary in Pompeii. This unusual shrine is a rare representation of Mt Vesuvius before the eruption of 79 AD.*

▨ *Personification of the Deities* ▨

The Greeks contributed more than any other culture to the personalities of the different gods. Romans became used to identifying their gods with the Greek gods of Olympus. Thus Jupiter was identified with Zeus, the king of the Greek pantheon, Juno with Hera, the sister/wife of Zeus, and Minerva with Athena. In no case was the characterisation a really perfect match and Romans had to adapt the nature of their gods to fit with Greek concepts. Yet the trend towards synchronised religious system continued. This was not a rapid development but a slow acculturation over many centuries, though at times the assimilation was much faster and more dramatic.

▨ *Peace Treaty with the Gods* ▨

All "cities" had to maintain close contact with the countryside, their source of food and wealth. The more good farmland a state controlled, the more prosperous it was. In a land as rich as much of Italy, the belief that Nature was good and bountiful could flourish. It was easy to believe that the same gods who preserved a family and granted a fertile harvest also determined a nation's success in battle. When harvests failed and battles were lost, communities felt that angry gods needed to be placated. Each god was owed its special rituals, whether they were mystic races, equestrian displays, games or processions.

The Romans respected all gods. Their relationship with the divine and the benefits they provided was summarised by the *pax deorum*, the Peace Treaty with the gods. This was an "arrangement" whereby all due honour was paid to the gods and the gods assisted the Romans both by continuing the prosperity of Italy and success in the Imperial endeavours of the Roman people. If an enemy nation appeared to have a stronger god, the Romans had a ritual whereby the god was invited to Rome and promised a better deal and more honour from them than he or she was receiving in his or her native lands. If there was plague or other disaster, Rome might send for and consecrate an appropriate god from another country. If a forest had to be cut down, special prayers were said to propitiate the spirits of the trees so that the family would

14

not have to cope with unfriendly homeless spirits. If the Romans wanted to wage war, certain priests had to examine the situation and decide whether the Romans fought justly and therefore had the right to the approval of the gods. Ritual had to be exact and reverent. Any sign of a mistake meant that the whole had to be repeated — nothing must interfere with the proper order.

▼ *The countryside had its specific gods: Pan, the woodland god, spirits of water and trees, and Silenus, the spirit of wild life. This relief from Ostia Antica shows Silenus burning a sacrifice at a small altar. He wears a garland as part of his ritual dress and stands with an attitude of simple respect. Other Sileni were usually not quite so demure.*

▩ *Bridge Builders to the Gods* ▩

As well as augurs, the Romans had priestly colleges of *pontifices*. A *pontifex*, literally, was a "bridge builder" to the gods. He managed the ritual sacrifices which constituted the Roman People's side of the treaty. In addition, there were three *flamines*, religious officials dedicated to three significant gods: Jupiter, Mars and Quirinus, the name for Romulus, the city's founder, after he had been taken up to Heaven.

Members of priestly colleges and other religious officials came from the same prominent families who provided the politicians and generals. Julius Caesar, the conqueror of Gaul, was for much of his life *pontifex maximus*, that is, leader of the State religion. All Roman magistrates had a role in the pact with the gods. Consuls and praetors who led armies had to "take the auspices", that is, read the auguries or signs, and make prayers on behalf of the people.

▼ *Pompeii had its share of temples to the emperor. This altar is from the temple of Vespasian (69–79 AD) which had formerly served as a temple of Augustus. It shows a priest with his toga covering his head officiating at the sacrifice of a bull.*

▨ *Idealisation of Country Life* ▨

Long after Rome had become a city of a million people, poets and painters idealised the beauty of the Italian landscape and extolled the moral goodness of a simple country life. The Roman citizen ideally divided his time between fighting for his city, farming his land, and worshipping the gods of his household and the community with the correct ritual. His wife provided the household with clothing and managed the farm alongside her husband. The figure of the Sabine peasant tilling his plot of land surrounded by his children and sacrificing on a simple altar of turf was especially dear.

▼ *The countryside around Tusculum, to the south of Rome. Tusculum was in the Sabine territory which was famous in Roman tradition for producing the tough, honest hard-working peasants whose fighting prowess and virtues formed the backbone of Empire.*

Augustus — Bridge Builder to the Heavens

The shattering period of civil war (49 BC–29 BC) had coincided with displays of wealth and avarice. When Augustus Caesar grasped control of government in 27 BC his justification was expressed in religious terms. The peace with the gods had obviously been broken; how else would such a terrible experience have occurred? Romans, he said, had to renew their commitment to the proper observance of the gods. They had to turn their backs on luxury and regain their links with pristine Italy. He boasted that his wife, Livia, the most powerful woman in the Roman world, spun the material for his clothes as women had done in early legend. Temples were restored and religious ritual fostered.

The message was powerful. Italy united under Augustus' leadership. Ancient rituals were restored, even when people no longer remembered what they were for. The poet Ovid described many. One of the more curious was dedicated to Robigus, the god of rust in wheat. The *flamen* of Quirinus sacrificed a sheep and a dog and addressed the god. The message was simple: "Robigus, you do not have to prove anything to us. We are well aware of your ability to wreak destruction. Keep your scabby hands off the crops. We are happy to worship you but infinitely prefer to do so in your absence."

◀ Augustus, the first emperor of the Roman new order, based his claim to power partly on his right relationship with the gods. This statue, found in the Via Labicana in Rome, shows Augustus as Pontifex, literally bridge builder, one of the priests of the Roman State religion.

Augustus did more than resurrect ancient forgotten rituals. He centred religious practice upon himself and his family. The peoples of the East had grown used to worshipping their rulers. Slowly this became accepted in Italy also. After all, was not Augustus the man who had saved Italy from destruction and restored peace? Gradually Augustus and his family became the means by which the pact with the gods would be maintained. Without him, there would be no prosperity, no success, no tranquillity. The Imperial cult developed by degrees but became the central focus of religion in Rome and Italy. This was extended. Whatever religions a province of the Empire had, the worship of the emperor was incorporated within it.

Vines and olives need peace and time to grow. Harvest festivals need freedom from wars and time to enjoy them. The Empire of Rome restricted war to other parts of the world. The emperor as guardian of the Roman People, chief bridge builder to the heavens, ensured that the great endeavours of armies and the fertility of the land were permanently protected.

◀ *P. Vergilius Maro, (70–19 BC) was Rome's greatest epic poet. His pastoral poems sang the beauty of country life and peasant virtues. In his epic, the* Aeneid, *he reworked the foundation legends of Rome to suit the times in which he lived.*

The Myth of Aeneas, Prince of Troy

In the Age of Augustus, the first sole ruler of Rome since the exile of the kings, the story of Aeneas became very popular. Its greatest retelling was the epic, Aeneid, *written by Virgil, who lived through the civil wars and saw the triumph of Augustus. Virgil's Aeneas, obedient to the gods, was the vehicle through which Rome's destiny would be achieved. His story would be the link between Rome and the rich tradition of Greek epic. Aeneas, the founder of the Julian clan from which Augustus traced his descent, was also a person who could desert Dido and be the cause of turmoil and war in Italy. This complex characterisation reflects the mixed emotions of a poet who had seen both the destruction of Italy and the restoration and peace brought about by the victor.*

When Troy fell to the Greek armies at the end of the ten year war, most of the Trojan royal family was slaughtered. One of its number, Aeneas, son of Anchises and Venus, the goddess of love, escaped. He carried his aged father on his shoulders and the household gods of Troy in his arms. Close by him was his son Iulus Ascanius. His wife Creusa was lost in the turmoil of the burning city. Aeneas escaped with the remnants of the Trojans, determined to found a new Troy wherever the gods would decide.

The goddess Juno had always hated the Trojans. She favoured the Greeks so was determined to destroy Aeneas and his people. Venus, however, extracted a promise from Jupiter, the King of Heaven and Juno's husband, that whatever his wife attempted, the ragged band of refugees would eventually come to Italy and found a great nation. Even Juno, Venus said, would be won over to the inexorable destiny of their descendants.

Aeneas and his followers suffered many adventures on their way. Venus ensured they found a chance to rest when they landed in Africa where Queen Dido, a widow, was building her new city of Carthage. Venus contrived that the queen fall in love with her handsome son. Aeneas fell in love too and became Dido's consort although no marriage took place.

After a very short time, Jupiter sent his messenger Mercury to summon Aeneas to his destiny in Italy. He obeyed the command but tragic Dido, who could not bear her loss, threw herself on her funeral pyre rather than live. Aeneas looked back from his ship to see the smoke but only discovered in the context of a later adventure, his voyage to the underworld, that she had died.

The Trojans landed in Italy and were welcomed by the king of the Latins, Latinus, and Evander, the descendant of the Greeks who had settled in the area. Latinus offered his daughter Lavinia to Aeneas as a wife and Aeneas accepted the offer. But Juno was not finished yet. She stirred up the anger of the local prince Turnus, who had been betrothed to Lavinia before the arrival of the Trojan hero, and Lavinia's mother who also preferred Turnus to Aeneas. Soon Italy was at war and Aeneas had to defeat and kill his rival before he could take his place as the heir of the king.

Aeneas achieved all his aims partly through placating Juno by special sacrifices on the site which one day would be Rome and partly through the magnificent armour which Venus asked her husband Vulcan to make for her son. The gods were reconciled, the Trojans had found a home, Lavinia a husband descended from the gods, and the future Romans a heritage that linked them to the divine.

"I am a citizen of Rome"

❖ Registration — the Census ❖

Every five years, each who was eligible to be a citizen of Rome had to stand before the two censors, senior statesmen elected for this purpose, and state his name, age, income, military service, marital status, tribe and the number of his children. His ability to give a satisfactory answer to these questions first led to conferment and then confirmation of his citizenship, that is, his membership of the Roman People, his right to decide legislation and elect magistrates and to be protected by Roman law, his duty to defend the state to the limit of his capacity and to obey legitimate authorities. The censors judged his moral fitness and recorded his income. They assigned him to a century, a military classification based on property, and a tribe, which identified him as part of the Roman community.

▼ This relief depicts the Roman census with its attached ritual sacrifice. It dates between 35–32 BC and was built by L. Domituis Ahenobarbus, a supporter of Antony and, incidentally, the great grandfather of the emperor Nero.

22

▲ *The Roman Forum, located between the Capitoline and Palatine Hills, was originally a marsh which, when drained, formed the original site of Rome. It was the centre of civic, mercantile, legal and religious activity through the Republican period.*

▨ *Voting in Groups* ▨

Rome began as a tiny city state surrounded by farmland. Its citizens were its male soldiers and farmers. Some of its customs retained a small-scale mentality even after it grew into the largest city in the ancient world. A Roman had to be in Rome to vote. He voted not as an individual but as a member of a group. In military affairs, he joined his century. Each century cast a vote. There were 193 centuries strictly ranked according to wealth. The richer centuries had fewer members and voted first. All the landless were registered in the bottom century and rarely had to vote.

▓ *The Assembly of the Tribes* ▓

The Assembly of the Tribes met to decide everything which was not military. There were thirty five tribes. Four of these were "urban", and thirty one were "rural". The rural tribes had two advantages: there were more of them and fewer people were registered in them. As time passed, the original association with a place of residence disappeared. A man inherited his tribal designation from his father. Others gained citizenship as adults and the censors decided their tribe. Censors could and did "rig" the vote by moving their supporters into rural tribes. Gerrymanders of all kinds were possible. Even so the Tribal Assembly was still more "democratic" than the centuries.

▓ *Inclusive Citizenship* ▓

Rome rejected the normal Mediterranean attitude of exclusive citizenship. For most of its history, citizenship was extended to individuals and communities. Slaves when they were freed became citizens, even though they were restricted to the urban tribes to limit their influence. Legends attest an infant city which welcomed immigrants and held to an ideal of social mobility based on merit. As Rome became the dominant power in the Mediterranean, there eventually developed an elite class and an attitude that Romans formed an exclusive "master race". However, there were always ways of joining the "master race" both through wealth and achievement.

◀ *M. Tullius Cicero (106–43 BC) was a statesman and author of works on rhetoric, philosophy, religion and politics. Our knowledge of late Republican history, in which he played a decisive role, largely depends upon Cicero's published works and collections of letters.*

Rome and Italy

Before Rome dominated Italy, there were several independent nations who saw little in common with each other. The great Etruscan culture of central Italy competed with the Greek communities of the south. Alongside them existed hill tribes such as the Samnites. Closest to the Romans were the peoples of Latium (Latins), regarded traditionally as related. Rome eventually brought all these people under her control with a series of alliances. The Latins had special rights at Roman law. Some of the Latin communities were granted full citizen rights very early in Roman history. Tusculum in 381 BC was such a community, Arpinum in 188 was another. Cicero, one of Rome's greatest literary and political figures, was born in Arpinum. He expressed a love and loyalty for both his native community and for Rome. His experience of a double homeland (patria) was shared by many.

▼ *The goddess of peace and fertility is pictured on the Altar of Augustan Peace, finished in 9 BC to celebrate the return of Augustus from foreign wars. In many respects, the Augustan Peace celebrates a return of prosperity to Italy which had been devastated by civil war since 91 BC.*

▣ *Rome's Italian Allies Demand the Citizenship* ▣

As her Imperial power extended, Rome grew reluctant to hand out citizenship to Italian communities. By the end of the second century BC Rome had completed her conquest of Italy and controlled a Mediterranean empire. Roman arrogance grew with success. The desire to guard privilege sharpened. The gap between citizens and allies grew wider although the allies still contributed half the soldiers to every Roman army. Bitterness and resentment at this led to the Social War fought against the allies (*socii*) throughout Italy from 90–89 BC. Some allies demanded citizenship. Others wanted to ditch Rome and form a new nation, *Italia*.

The military victory did go to Rome but the moral victory belonged to the Italians. Rome acknowledged their claims by offering citizenship to all Italians south of the Po River. Even so, the ensuing arguments over the effective registration of new citizens went on for nearly forty years and were a major factor in the final destruction of the Roman Republic.

The policy of expanding citizenship was established, although conservatives constantly bemoaned the "weakening" of Roman stock. Italians beyond the Po River were next to receive the vote. Gades (Cadiz) in Spain was the first community outside Italy to gain citizenship for all its inhabitants. There followed extensions to the Greek communities in Sicily. Grants to individuals continued throughout the Empire. These were not token gestures. New citizens were absorbed into the fabric of civic life. Eventually even emperors could be born outside Italy.

▣ *To Be Roman ...*▣

One side effect of this successful policy was the mixing of several cultures. Local custom outside Rome remained but appeared submerged. Over centuries a process of "Romanisation" affected the whole Roman Empire. This was not only "the spread of civilisation". It meant the transformation of many cultures and the establishment of a "norm" by which outsiders could be judged. Rome itself was transformed through interaction with its provinces. To be "Roman" had less and less association with the city or Italy. It became a powerful idea with a life of its own.

▨ *The Individual and the State* ▨

The citizen of Rome ideally believed that his existence lay in serving his community, by his efforts to defend it, by his contribution to its economic well-being, by his participation in community religious practices, and by his procreation of the next generation of citizens. The more a person could do these things, the more honour was his due.

Citizens were not considered equal because it was thought they did not contribute equally in either talent or wealth. But every citizen had basic rights: his three part Roman name, the right to wear the toga, or citizen dress, to vote for legislation and for his annual leaders, and the right of appeal to the People. From 167 BC, the Roman citizen did not pay direct tax. Tax was for subject peoples. He benefited at certain times from grain subsidies and even handouts. Women were citizens in that they were recognised members of the Roman community and were protected by Roman law, but they had access to neither the privileges nor the duties of males.

▨ *A Proud People* ▨

The Romans were proud. *"Libertas"* meant freedom to choose one's leaders and not to call anyone king or master. Even the Roman custom of patronage was understood within these terms. A patron earned his right to deference by the services he provided for his client; a client paid respect to his patron because he thought him worthy of it. *Fides*, good faith, was the bond between them, not law. If a patron let his client down, the client could attach himself to a new patron. Or he could appeal to the "public patron", the tribune of the plebs.

▶ *"On the Ides of March" — this proud slogan coinmemorates the assassination of Julius Caesar on 15th March, 44 BC by his associates who believed he destroyed the Roman "Libertas", freedom. The cap in the centre is that worn by freed slaves.*

▨ *The Right of Appeal* ▨

Roman society was divided into two castes, Patricians and Plebeians. In early Roman history, only patricians could become military leaders, only patricians knew the law, only patricians consulted the gods on behalf of the state. The plebeians fought in the armies, voted in the assemblies and paid taxes. The consul, like his forerunner the king, could put a citizen to death without a trial or have him beaten on the spot. The symbol of his power was the *fasces*, twelve bundles of rods and an axe which his attendants could use whenever he ordered it.

Once the kings were exiled, plebeians wanted to end patrician domination as well as monarchy. They first demanded their own representatives, the tribunes of the plebs, who would protect them from the consul's power. These ten annually elected officers had the right to veto any action of a Roman magistrate except in very rare circumstances. When a citizen appealed to a tribune for help, he would dramatically place himself between the victim and the attendants. The consul could not touch the sacred body of the tribune. The principle of appeal to the people and its representatives against oppression was fundamental to the Roman concept of freedom.

◀ *Roman voting had always been carried out openly until the 130s BC, when laws were passed which allowed each voter to cast a secret ballot. The laws broke the power of the great patron who thought he had a right to make sure his client voted the right way.*

Plebeian Victories

Plebeians eventually won the right to attain all civil and military offices, most religious positions and to make laws. They did this by going on strike. They outnumbered the patricians so drastically that when they left the city boundaries and demanded change before they would return, the patricians had to capitulate. Patricians retained the right to lead senatorial debate and monopolised some major priesthoods. They still had a superior social status. But this was all. The Roman social order changed. A new elite emerged which based its claims to honour on merit, not birth. This was the *nobilitas*, or the "well-known" group which consisted of descendants, whether patrician or plebeian, of those who had been elected to the highest public office, the consulship, not men born into a particular caste.

The Nobilitas — an Open Elite

In the annual election of magistrates, the members of the *nobilitas* had advantages of fame and wealth. However, their ranks were not closed. The governing class of Rome continually accepted outsiders of "suitable" background and mentality to its ranks. If a "new" man

▶ *Glory was an important ambition of every Roman, especially for those families whose men could look forward to an illustrious career. These men were commemorated by wax masks which their families could display, as this man does in a statue found at Ostia, west of Rome.*

29

such as Cicero had the talent, wealth and tenacity to impress the Roman voters in the several elections of his public career, he might win his place among the highest. Few went to the top in one generation, but a man who got part way up the ladder might produce descendants who surpassed him. Nor could the *nobilitas* regard their position as secure. Descendants of consuls, along with the rest, had to be elected for each office on the ladder. Families with a high profile in one century could die out and disappear in a later one.

The Roman People — Part of the Government

The assembled Roman People of the Republican period was an integral part of the constitutional process. It voted on laws and to elect magistrates. It decided whether Rome would go to war or make peace. The magistrates were expected to respect its "greaterness" or *maiestas*. Not to do so was treason. The *maiestas* of the People was eventually dramatised when the consul agreed to lower the *fasces* in the people's assemblies and to remove the axe from the bundle when the magistrate was inside the city. The People was expected to honour the magistrates whom it had elected as long as they honoured the people and the law.

Not a Democracy

Rome never was and never became a democracy. Some tribunes of the plebs demanded that more recognition be given to the people. But even they had a limited idea of what was "democratic". At public meetings only magistrates, tribunes, or specially selected representatives could speak. The individual was restricted to heckling. The principle of voting in groups made the individual less powerful, particularly if he were a member of a crowded urban tribe or the bottom century. Secret ballot, introduced in stages between 139 and 119 BC, at least stopped the domination of a patron "checking" a vote, but patronage continued to allow powerful individuals to exercise their influence.

Split between Government and People

At the same time that trouble was brewing among Rome's Italian allies, a savage split developed between government and people. *"Libertas"*

◀ *Two coins from the late 2nd century BC pick up on the hotly debated issues of the day. One was whether grain should be subsidised by the State, the other concerned the rights of patrons to check out how their supporters actually voted. The first coin recalls the narrow bridges which prevented the powerful from looking over voters' shoulders. Depicted in the second coin are two officials commemorating the issue of grain by the Senate.*

became associated with opposition to the established government of Rome. The Social War was not quite over when civil war broke out in 88 BC and continued until 81. Even after this, many problems in Rome and throughout Italy were left to smoulder. When civil war broke out again in 49 BC it did so mostly because these problems had never been resolved. Civil war led to the establishment of an emperor, a return to monarchy.

▦ *When the People Assumed Force* ▦

The Roman citizen of the last years of the Republic suffered deep social change. At this time, some citizens formed gangs to take "direct action" such as street riots. They believed this was more effective than exercising legitimate citizen rights. Force became more important than any electoral process. The cost was high.

Once one man assumed control, the Roman People was no longer sovereign. The emperor Tiberius transferred elections to the Senate. The citizen still received his grain dole, entertainment, and could riot if he was unhappy, but he no longer decided directly who was to govern him

▲ *On the South Frieze of the Altar of Augustan Peace, the Senate and priestly colleges of Rome are pictured in solemn and reverent procession. Note the strange, pointed hats of the Flamines, special priests of Rome; and the togas of the priests covering their heads in the presence of the gods.*

or how. Citizenship was still a mark of distinction and carried legal privilege but birth was far more significant. A citizen could appeal to Caesar in place of the now defunct tribune, but had to have the resources to make his appeal heard.

▨ *Citizenship Equals Power* ▨

Emperors used citizenship as a means of spreading Roman power. Local leaders were made citizens and they would then keep local communities under control. Men who served in the auxiliary legions would eventually be rewarded with citizenship. The trend towards a "common *patria*" continued. In 212 AD the emperor Caracalla granted suffrage throughout the Roman Empire. The ideal of a privileged citizen group was lost and a new scheme of things, whereby there was one law for the rich and honourable and another for the poor and powerless, was in place.

▲ *This detail of the South Frieze of the Altar of Augustan Peace shows a new trend in political life. Now, along with the Senate, priests and magistrates, is the Imperial Household including the women and children of Augustus' family.*

▲ *The West Frieze of the Altar of Augustan Peace shows Father Aeneas sacrificing on the site which would become Rome. Augustus pictured himself as the new founder who renewed Rome after the civil war period.*

The Myth of Romulus and Remus
— the Founders of Rome

Like Aeneas, Romulus was an ambivalent figure in Roman legend. He established a great city and founded the king's council of elders, the Senate. But he was a king and the Romans learned to hate kings. And he had killed his brother. When civil war was shattering the Roman people's confidence, they remembered the ancient fratricide and it weighed heavily on their collective conscience. But in most periods of Roman history, Romulus, the son of the war god Mars, chief priest and interpreter of the will of Heaven, founder of The City, was happily worshipped as the god Quirinus by the Quirites, the citizen body of Rome.

The son of Aeneas, Ascanius Iulus, founded the city of Alba Longa and had ruled it well. But his descendants suffered misfortune. King Numitor had been deposed by his brother Amulius. So that Numitor's only surviving child, Rhea Silvia, would produce no heirs, Amulius dedicated her to the goddess Vesta as a Vestal Virgin. If she broke the vow of virginity while in the service of the goddess she would suffer dreadful punishment.

Mars, the god of war, fell in love with the priestess. By him she conceived twin sons, Romulus and Remus. Her uncle imprisoned her and the children she bore were put on the banks of the river Tiber to die. They were saved by a she-wolf who suckled them until they were found by the shepherd Faustulus who raised the twins as his own sons.

The boys grew up and became leaders of the local shepherds against the local bandits. The bandits laid a trap for them and Remus was captured and handed over to the king. Romulus saved him. Their uncle was overthrown, their grandfather restored to power and their identity revealed. The princes now took their place as members of the royal family.

Both men had the desire to found their own city on the site where they had been miraculously saved by the wolf. They marked out the site and invited their former fellow shepherds, robbers, thieves and bandits to join them. To decide who would rule they read the heavens to discover the will of the gods. Six vultures appeared to Remus on the Aventine Hill, twelve vultures to Romulus on the Palatine. Remus claimed that he had seen the birds first, Romulus that he had seen a greater number. A quarrel broke out and in the anger of the moment, Romulus killed Remus. Romulus named the city "Roma" after himself.

His followers needed women to marry. Romulus asked the families of the nearby towns whether they would consider marrying some of their daughters to the Romans. The local peoples were disgusted by the thought. But they agreed nonetheless to come to a festival in Rome. At the festival, Romulus gave the signal and his Romans snatched and carried away as many women as they could find and made them their wives.

The fiercest people who had attended the festival were the Sabines. They fought to regain their daughters and by treachery gained control of the Roman citadel. The Romans prepared for a bloody all-out battle. In the midst of the fighting, the women took action. They rushed onto the battlefield and stopped the fighting. The Romans had offered them honourable marriage, they said. Some of them now had children. If the Romans and Sabines fought they would lose either husbands and the fathers of their babies on the one hand or brothers and fathers on the other. The men saw the point and ceased. They agreed to join as one people and the Sabine king, Titius Tatus, and Romulus agreed to rule jointly.

35

"I came, I saw, I conquered"

Senatus Populus-Que Romanus — the Senate and the People of Rome

More than anything else, Rome was a military culture. In its early period, the citizen-farmer who owned a certain amount of land was a reality. This image remained as an ideal. The Senate and magistrates led the people in war, the people served as soldiers.

A proper Roman of any class boasted of his *virtus,* his moral and physical courage. The word comes from the Latin for "man", *vir.* The English words "virile" and "virtue" give two aspects of its meaning. A man of *virtus* was by nature courageous, willing to fight desperate wars defending Rome and extending its power into other areas. He gave to the state according to his means and the state rewarded him according to his contribution. Allied states also provided cohorts according to their treaty obligations. Roman citizen and Italian ally fought together to establish Roman supremacy first in Italy and then throughout the Mediterranean world.

The Military Hierarchy

A soldier could make his way up the ranks to the post of first centurion. Roman officers came from the wealthy. They commanded both the citizen and allied legions. Young Romans were meant to serve ten campaigns before they could stand for public office. They might start as young as sixteen years of age. They then had to be elected to the posts of military tribune, quaestor, aedile, praetor and consul. They were usually elected to a senior post only after holding those less important.

This ladder was known as the *cursus honorum*, the race for honours. In this *cursus* the aedile alone had no military duties but administered urban concerns such as water supplies and entertainments. Junior posts outnumbered senior. The consuls were the supreme military leaders as well as chief civil magistrates. Only two were elected each year amid cut throat competition.

When Rome's theatres of war outstripped the number of consuls, the Senate created pro-consuls. A brilliant military career was the surest way to win political success. Individual glory accrued and brought

▶ *C. Julius Caesar, (c.104–44 BC) is perhaps the most famous Roman of all. He was on the losing side of the civil wars of 88–81 BC but became dictator from 49 BC first for a short period then finally for life. His success depended on his military reputation, his manipulation of politics and a ground swell of dissatisfaction with the powers that be.*

37

collective honour to a family. The greatest proof of courage for a general was to be awarded a triumph, a huge victory procession through the streets of Rome followed by a feast for the Roman People. Imperator (general) and army were honoured on the day, but the Triumphator and his family commemorated such an event for generations.

▼ *A section of Trajan's column from 113 AD. Trajan pushed the limits of the Roman Empire into Dacia in campaigns of 101–102 and 105–106. This commemorative column in the heart of Rome tells the story of Trajan, his soldiers and the Dacian king Decebalus. It is a most important source for our knowledge of military life — and was also Trajan's tomb. The original statue of Trajan was replaced by one of St Peter.*

A "Common" Soldier's Story

One man's career tells us much of Republican military life and its ideals. In 171 BC the annual call up was under way. Because of the huge number of wars in which Rome had fought there were many men highly qualified as soldiers. Too many wanted to be centurions, the highest rank for an ordinary soldier. Those who were to be demoted appealed to the tribunes. One, Spurius Ligustinus, presented his case, and had probably been encouraged to do so by the consuls. Livy, writing at the time of Augustus, records his speech (Book 42.34):

I, Spurius Ligustinus of the Tribe of Crustumina, am of Sabine family. My father left me a tiny patch of land and a little hut. There I was born and raised and I live there today. As soon as I was old enough, my father gave me a wife, the daughter of his brother, who brought nothing with her but her free birth, her good reputation and a fertility which would have satisfied a wealthy house. We have six sons and two daughters, both married. Four sons wear their adult togas, two are still boys. I became a soldier while Sulpicius and Aurelius were consuls [200 BC]. I was taken to Macedonia for two years as a common soldier to fight King Philip; in the third year there, because of my courage, Flamininus made me junior centurion. When Philip and the Macedonians had been defeated, I immediately went to Spain with the consul Marcus Cato [195 BC]. This great general judged me worthy to be first centurion of the first century of hastati [front row]. When I volunteered for the third time I was sent to face the Aetolians and King Antiochus. I was first centurion in the first century of the main formation. King Antiochus was forced out of Greece and the Aetolians were beaten and we returned. Twice I campaigned in Spain with Fulvius Flaccus and then Sempronius Gracchus. I came back with Flaccus among those he selected for their courage to march in his Triumph. I went back because Gracchus asked for me. Four times within a few years I was chief centurion; thirty four times I have been rewarded by my generals for courage; I have earned six civic crowns. I have served twenty two years in the army and am more than fifty years old. I could claim exemption through age or through the four soldiers I could offer in my place. For my part, I prefer that while anyone forming an army thinks me fit for service, I should never be excused. Whatever rank the military tribunes think I ought to be is their decision. I shall make it my business that no other soldier surpasses me in courage. My generals and fellow soldiers will testify that I have always done so. And you, my comrades, although it is fair that you appeal since when you were serving you never did anything against the authority of the magistrates and the Senate, it is just that you yield to the power of the consul and the Senate and consider every rank honourable in which you are about to defend the State.

Ligustinus embodies an enduring ideal: patriotism and obedience to the authority of the consuls and the Senate bring just recognition and reward. An army of such soldiers hardly needed a general. Implied in the story is the belief that courage will be noticed by the general but also that service will not stop until the need has passed or the centurion was no longer capable of performing his duties.

Ligustinus' story helps us to understand the impact of Rome's growing empire on the peasant families of Italy. His tiny patch was in fact under the minimum requirement, but the need for soldiers was too great. He saw service in Greece, Macedonia and Spain. In the meantime, his wife was left to raise the children and keep the farm running as best she could. The booty from foreign wars was essential to their income. Behind the ideal was a harsh reality — soldiering brought in better money than farming. As soon as Rome stopped winning wars, soldiers like Ligustinus would, and did, suffer drastically.

As the second century BC progressed and Rome's wars in Spain drained the resources of state and individual, there were fewer men like

◀ *This grave relief commemorates Marcus Caelius who was killed with Quinctilius Varus and three legions in the Teutoberg Forest in 9 AD. Few survived the disaster. Caelius' family picture him with all his military decorations prominently displayed. His freemen, who are also commemorated, are pictured with him.*

Ligustinus prepared to enlist. In some cases there was not even a tiny patch of land awaiting their return. By the end of the century, the property qualification had completely disappeared. The move from citizen soldier to professional was under way.

Rome had acquired an empire through the blood and sweat of soldiers and their families. The usual reward had been booty and a land grant. Providing both became more difficult and generals needed to be successful politicians in order to satisfy their soldiers. Success in war, on the other hand, brought with it outstanding political influence if one could survive the political traps set by opponents.

A century after Ligustinus, Rome was in the throes of civil war. Two underlying causes of this war were the pressure placed on Roman government by the need to provide for soldiers and a failure to keep successful generals under control.

▲ *Triumphal arches across Europe are a visible reminder of Roman conquest. This arch is located at Orange in southern France.*

Soldiers and Politics

The great generals of the Late Republic also inherited an ideal. However, instead of wanting to be "worthy" of their families and the state, they wanted to be "the best". They also wanted to amass as large a fortune as possible. Fame and economics pushed Pompey into the East and Caesar to conquer Gaul and attempt the expeditions to Britain. To celebrate a triumph was an honour worth remembering even if you were a common soldier. To a general, it was a pinnacle. To triumph, as Pompey did, over three continents, made one an equal of Alexander. Caesar went one better. He held four triumphs over Gaul, Egypt, Asia and Africa.

▲ *The Triumphal Arch of Titus is one of the many memorials of Empire in Rome. Titus conquered Jerusalem in 70 AD and held his triumph in 71. He depicts the procession including the display of treasure from the Great Temple.*

These generals and others like them depended on their ordinary soldiers. They had to recruit them, sometimes relying on their personal appeal and reputation. The soldiers expected success and wealth. Generals who could deliver these were little short of gods. When they combined success with a reputation for bravery and leadership from the front, they were gods, as Caesar was regarded in the eyes of his men. Where he led them, they followed, on foot for the most part and carrying all they needed. When Caesar was assassinated in 44 BC, his veterans as a group demanded vengeance. Their voice was so loud that eventually no deal was possible between his assassins and the Caesarian supporters. Their influence was so great that if they decided Caesar's eighteen year old heir was important, then he was.

▶ This statue of Augustus was found at the villa of his wife, Livia, near the Prima Porta at Rome. Here Augustus is Imperator (general) addressing his troops. It was made after 20 BC. Its highly decorated breastplate commemorates the return of standards captured by Parthia in 53 BC in a major defeat. Although this was achieved by diplomatic settlement, Augustus represents it as a major victory achieved through the blessing of the gods.

▨ *Augustus' Army* ▨

Caesar's heir, Augustus, saw the need to reorganise both the soldiers and their generals. He had risen to power through the loyalty of the troops — no-one else was to be encouraged to do the same. He drastically reduced the number of legions and tied the remaining soldiers to himself and to his family by special privileges. What had previously been uncertain rewards to soldiers became systematised pensions organised by Augustus.

At the same time, generals had less opportunity for massive personal glory. Triumphs were gradually restricted to members of the Imperial family or men very closely aligned with it. Members of the Equestrian Order, that is wealthy non-senators, took on many military duties and even commanded the province of Egypt, because their loyalty and career prospects were directly linked to their relationship with the emperor.

The veterans had determined politics in the Late Republic — they could keep a person on the throne or put up a successor in later times. A good reputation with the army was an important element in any emperor's health. If, as with the emperor Trajan, the army thought highly of you, your reign had a good chance of surviving. If not, you might be lucky to last a few months. Rival soldiers fought to place "their" candidate in power. Those who were successful were richly rewarded. Even emperors with little or no military talent depicted themselves as courageous generals and made sure the soldiers were happy.

▨ *Empire and Army* ▨

The army became a means of spreading Roman values and customs. Around the Empire towns sprang up wherever there was a need for military camps or wherever veterans were settled in colonies. Men could become citizens through serving in auxiliary units; provincial peoples could form identifiable units in the army and would in this way travel the Empire. Although in the army of Imperial times soldiers could not legally marry until their period of service was over, they made lasting contracts with women in the provinces where they served. Through recruitment practices, intermarriage and the steady production of

▲ *The emperor Marcus Aurelius (161–180 AD) is usually remembered as a quiet, comtemplative man but he also had to lead armies and campaign extensively against invading tribes. His military images were as impressive as his philosophy, though not as well remembered.*

children, the army was, more than any other Roman institution, the vehicle which brought Rome to the outer reaches of the Empire and kept it there.

As provincial-born citizens were recruited, they brought back to the centre customs and ideas from their own communities. Less actual fighting was done. Defence of the borders became a major duty, as was building and maintenance. Generals still sought triumphs but soldiers were not so happy to fight for them. The soldiers of the emperor Claudius in Germany asked if he could simply award his general the triumph to save them the trouble of winning the war.

The spirit of Ligustinus, the common soldier, lived on but his counterparts in later centuries lived a very different life. The Roman soldier, with his reputation for toughness, efficiency, loyalty and courage became a symbol of all things Roman. Bridges, walls, aqueducts and roads are enduring monuments to the Roman presence and the sweat of the soldiers who built them.

▲ *Hadrian's Wall separated the Roman from the non-Roman world. It was built about 122 AD. Unlike his predecessor Trajan, Hadrian refused to add to the Empire. He concentrated the legions around the boundaries of the Empire and consciously strove to define the borders. The wall is an impressive reminder of this policy. It can still be traced even though much of the stone was recycled into local building projects.*

The Women Of Ancient Rome

In the *Aeneid*, his great epic telling of the foundation of Rome and her Trojan past, the poet Virgil paints for us many female characters: goddesses who mix feminine wiles with godlike power, loyal and selfless mortal women, powerful queens and prophetesses. These women introduce us to ideas about women and femininity common among the writers and thinkers of ancient Rome.

The mythological picture is complex, as is any study of women in ancient societies and particularly in Rome where women controlled wealth, but could not vote; where women wielded political influence but more usually served to connect male allies by marriage; where women could be saviours of the state though they induced in men a fear of what would happen if they got out of control.

▶ *Roman ladies of various periods went for curls, curls and more curls. This lady comes from the period of the Flavian emperors (69–96 AD). Even earlier the poet Ovid shows that the fashion for wigs was lucrative and popular. "A woman walks, her head laden down with bought tresses. She uses money to replace her old curls with new ones and doesn't even blush at the thought."* (Ars Amatoria 3.165.8–48)

48

🔳 *Women in Roman Legend* 🔳

Stories from Rome's legendary past tell of heroines and female villains as well as the great men and their enemies who brought fame to the growing city around the eighth to the sixth century BC. We find most of them, such as the story of Rome's legendary founder, Romulus and the Sabine women in the works of Livy, a historian writing at the time of Augustus (28 BC–14 AD).

Several generations after Romulus, a new king, Tarquinius Priscus, emerged in Rome. He was an Etruscan outsider whose success was foretold by his wife Tanaquil through her knowledge of divine signs. Tanaquil, though not always approved of, was a worthy queen to Tarquinius, one of Rome's great kings. She was a king maker in her own right, for when her husband was murdered, she engineered her son-in-law Servius Tullius into his place.

Tanaquil was a respected figure even though the idea of a woman having that much power caused a certain amount of discomfort in Roman authors.

🔳 *Tullia — the Wicked Princess* 🔳

The younger daughter of Servius Tullius was definitely a villain. In Livy's account of early Rome, Tullia, energetic, ambitious and unscrupulous, killed her own husband and her sister, then married her sister's husband called Tarquinius Superbus (the Arrogant). The evil pair successfully plotted the death of Tullia's father and the theft of his throne. There is no doubt who was worse in Livy's eyes, for although Tarquinius killed the old king, Tullia ordered her carriage to be driven over Servius' dead body (Livy 1.48):

> Everyone thinks Tullia set up the deed. This much is true
> enough: she was driven into the Forum and, unabashed by
> the crowd of men, she called her husband out of the Senate
> House and hailed him king. Fearing the turmoil,
> Tarquinius sent her home. On the way, her driver stopped
> in panic. Pulling on the reins, he pointed out to his mistress
> the body of her slaughtered father lying on the ground.

What happened next was disgraceful and inhuman. The
place itself, called "The Street of Crime", commemorates
the deed. For, they say, in a frenzy caused by the avenging
spirits of her sister and husband, Tullia drove over her dead
father's body. Her carriage was spattered with his blood
and she carried back this pollution to the household gods
she shared with Tarquinius.

It should come as no surprise that Tarquinius the Arrogant was Rome's
last king. Their son, Sextus Tarquinius, also full of tyrannical pride,
broke the laws of hospitality and guest friendship by forcing Lucretia,
the virtuous wife of one of his relatives, to have sex with him. Lucretia
appealed to her father and husband for revenge, then killed herself.
They responded by driving the kings from Rome and founding the
Roman Republic in 509 BC.

▨ *Women of Decorum* ▨

The legends of heroines and villains continue into the period of the
Republic. Cloelia was a young girl of noble birth who was taken
hostage by Lars Porsenna, an Etruscan king who tried to restore the

◀ *This lady died around 50 AD
in Egypt. She is pictured in her
rich, gold jewellery and her best
clothes. After the Roman
conquest of Egypt, we see a
merging of Roman culture with
the existing Graeco-Egyptian
habits. The combination of
cultures allows us insight into
the wealth and status of many
women in Roman Egypt.*

kings to Rome. She broke free and swam across the Tiber rather than stay in captivity. Cloelia was one of very few women to be honoured in Rome with a public statue.

Veturia, the mother of Gaius Marcius Coriolanus, induced him to stop his attack on the city. According to Plutarch's biography of Coriolanus (from which Shakespeare's play derives) a grateful Roman Senate offered his mother and her companions any honour they wished. When they asked only to be allowed to commemorate their achievement by dedicating a temple to Womanly Fortune, they made claim to the female virtue of pudicitia, a right sense of place and decorum.

Tarpeia — Villain of Legend

Perhaps the most famous villain of early legend was Tarpeia, a young girl who, dazzled by the golden bracelets of Rome's Sabine enemies, agreed to betray the city to them if they would give her "what was on their left arm". When they were let in, they killed the girl with their shields, carried, along with the bracelets, on their left arms. A rock at the northern end of the Forum from which traitors and other criminals were cast was named after her as a reminder of her perfidy.

Control of Women

In a thousand years of Roman history, conditions of life changed often. Differences of economic and social status, region, and political climate make the picture one of immense diversity. Despite the fact that women of different character and background lived very different lives, some points of law and social practice did remain reasonably constant throughout Roman history.

Socially, women could use strategies to become wealthy and powerful. However, there was a deep cultural belief that women ought to be controlled, and legislation was put in place to ensure limits to the size of their inheritance and to restrict their business ventures. Thus much of the achievement of women in ancient Rome lay in finding means to subvert the legal system and cultural bias.

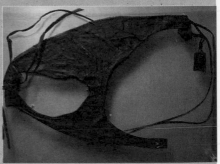

▲ *Great villas around the Roman world were decorated with magnificent mosaic floors. This floor of a 3rd–4th century villa in Sicily shows a woman about to be crowned for athletic success. A fellow victor stands beside her. Women competed in leather bikini-like costumes. The remains of this one (right) were found in London.*

▨ The Power of the Father ▨

Every citizen family in Rome or the Empire where Roman law operated was ruled by the *pater familias*, the father of the household. This man had the right of life and death over his legitimate children, male and female, until his death. He was master of all the slaves belonging to that household and controlled all wealth produced by it. His children were dependent on him while he lived unless a complicated legal procedure released them from his legal power. The daughters of the household were thus part of a web of control emanating from the father/master; the female slaves of the household were completely under their master's control; freedwomen owed a debt of gratitude to the controller of the household for granting their freedom.

▶ *Livia Drusilla was the wife of Augustus from 39 BC until his death in 14 AD. Augustus married her for her brains as well as her family connections. They had no children so Livia spent much energy on securing power for her sons by her earlier marriage against the claims of Augustus' relatives.*

▶ *The Severan dynasty of the 3rd century AD had as many powerful women as the Antonines or the Julio-Claudians. Julia Domna, the wife of the founder of the dynasty, was a Syrian. She maintained her power even when one of her sons killed the other.*

▨ *Marriage* ▨

Girls were usually married soon after they reached puberty, perhaps between thirteen and eighteen years of age, to a man chosen by her father who usually acted in consultation with his relatives and close friends.

Most Roman wives stayed within the economic and legal structures of their father's household even while living and becoming an integral part of their husbands'. This had not always been the case.

In very early times it had been customary to transfer a newly married woman from the power of the father to that of the husband. In her new home, the wife's legal status was "in place of a daughter" in her husband's house — thus he had similar power over her as he would have over his daughters and she would have inheritance rights which equalled her daughters.

This form of marriage became unpopular though never extinct. Most women we know of underwent the simpler form of marriage where the father's power remained in place. To emphasise the legal reality, a wife was required to spend three nights a year away from her husband's house. If she did not, she came under his legal power as she would have done in early Roman society.

❈ *On Her Father's Death* ❈

While her father lived, he controlled a woman's economic activity and her life. A father could divorce his daughter from her husband without their consent if he thought fit, though custom would require him to have reason to do so. Once he died, however, a woman did not automatically pass into the power of her husband or any particular male relative, such as a son. She was heir as her brothers were to her father's estate but with one complication: from this point all her business and other transactions depended upon the consent of her *tutor* or legal guardian. However, as time passed, the woman gained more control over selecting a tutor and could get rid of one who got in the way.

With the consent of a willing *tutor*, and as long as her father was dead, a woman could run a business, make investments, draw up a legally binding will, own slaves and run a household — she could even become overwhelmingly rich.

So although a woman was a partner to her husband, she was not usually economically dependent on him. Her husband certainly had use of the profit from her dowry but in the event of divorce, the principal was returned to her father if he were living, or to herself if her father was dead. In this respect she was no worse off than her brothers, who also came under the legal power of their father and were economically dependent on him while he lived.

◀ *The fashion of the sculptors from the Hellenistic East came to Rome. One facet of this was an interest in old people. This woman from Ostia makes no apologies for being old. Her respectable status is shown by her neat hairstyle and veiled head.*

▥ *Equality in Divorce* ▥

Divorce was frequent and common in most periods of Roman history. A woman, if free of her father's power, had as equal a right as her husband to end the marriage. Even women whose fathers still lived can be seen to have had far more say in the choice of a second or third husband than did the young girl of fourteen or fifteen. Thus, the older a woman became, the more her opinion counted. If wealth and successful motherhood were added, a matron could become a power to be reckoned with in the tightly knit social world of ancient Rome.

▥ *Control by Social Means* ▥

In order for a man to control his wife as Roman custom expected of him he used social as well as legal means. One significant control lay in the fact that all children of the marriage belonged to him. He chose whether or not they were to be raised, and in the event of divorce, the children lived on in his household. Normal social custom gave the mother access to the children as well as a say in their future. If he had the consent of her father, a husband could beat his wife for such transgressions as getting drunk, and he was certainly expected to act if adultery were proved against her. In this event, he had the right to retain part of her dowry as his own.

A henpecked husband was a figure for comedy and satire, a dominating wife a subject for propagandists and moralists who claimed her as a sign of the degeneracy of the individual concerned or the state in general.

▥ *The Naming of Women* ▥

One indication of the underlying legal and cultural attitude towards women in Rome was the fact that they did not possess personal names. Tanaquil and the women of Etruria did, but not the "Roman" Tullia. "Tullia" is merely the female form of her family name, Tullius. Her murdered sister's name was exactly the same. To distinguish between the two, the elder was called "Tullia Major", the younger, "Tullia Minor". If there were more than two, they would bear the Latin equivalents of "Tullia One, Tullia Two, Tullia Three..." and so on.

▦ *"The Ideal Family"* ▦

There was a rich tradition in Rome of the ideal family, of partnership between husband and wife, of devotion and love between parents and children. There are anecdotes about women's involvement in important family decisions, of raising children and carrying the family in the event of a husband's death or absence.

Roman mothers had a reputation for controlling their sons. The mother of Rome's reforming tribunes of 133 and 123–1 BC, Cornelia, was praised for the way she reared her sons even by those who violently disagreed with their politics.

Tombstones as well as authors of poetry and history attest the ideal of a supportive family structure and conjugal harmony.

▦ *Women in Control* ▦

Political turmoil, especially civil war, could place women in grave danger of losing all, but it also gave new opportunities for those who wanted them for seizing power and making a fortune. Moralists of the late Republican period lamented the amount of freedom and economic activity afforded women by the confusion of the times.

During the civil wars of 49–30 BC, women had to defend their own interests and those of their menfolk by whatever means were at hand. Hortensia, daughter of one of Rome's greatest orators, made a speech in the Forum demanding that a special civil war tax on women be dropped. She at least had the number of women affected cut down by a considerable figure. Servilia,

◀ *Agrippina the Younger, great granddaughter of the emperor Augustus, became the fourth wife of the emperor Claudius in order to secure power for her son. She was the most openly powerful of the Imperial women of her time but was eventually murdered by Nero.*

◀ *Plotina, wife of the emperor Trajan, actively assisted him in the running of the Roman Empire and was instrumental in the selection of his successor Hadrian. Hadrian deified both Trajan and Plotina.*

the mother of Caesar's assassin Brutus and formidable throughout her life, was able to change an insulting senatorial decree concerning the fate of her son and son-in-law by "backroom" methods. Fulvia, wife of Mark Antony, vigorously defended his interests when he was down and spurred him onto greater action when he was succeeding. She died in 40 BC but not before rallying his supporters into a war which nearly saw the defeat of his opponent Octavian (Augustus). It took the wealth and resources of Cleopatra, queen of Egypt, to give him a second, and still unsuccessful, chance in 31 BC at the Battle of Actium.

🔲 *The Backlash* 🔲

The era of Augustus (28 BC–AD 14) saw changes in the legal status of women which had both good and bad effects. In his efforts to settle the state after three generations of civil war, Augustus satisfied the moralists and attempted to put women "back in their place". New laws were passed, outlawing adultery and enforcing remarriage in the event of divorce or widowhood. Social mores reinforced the "norm" of respectability and submissiveness.

On the other hand, women who "did the right thing" and produced legitimate children were rewarded with legal and economic independence. A free-born woman who had had three children (and whose father was dead) and a freed slave woman who had borne four was no longer required to have a *tutor*. Augustus had first granted this right to his wife Livia and his sister Octavia. Both women were important in the Augustan regime, as role models and advisers.

This independence was taken up and utilised by generations of working women in the Imperial period to make their fortunes and achieve status within their own communities.

Women and Religion

There were many ways in which women participated in the religious experiences of the Romans, some acceptable (even commendable), many not. The Roman household itself was a rich centre of ritual connected with daily life, and the women of the household played their part.

Certain state magistracies of the Republican period entailed rituals to be carried out for the good of the community. It was the duty of the particular magistrate's wife to ensure this was done with absolute correctness. Wives of certain special priests (*flamines*) had specific duties and a special title, as did the wife of Rome's chief priest, the *pontifex maximus*.

The Greek Cult of Bacchus

Roman society could allow power and some independence to women as long as it was visible and controllable. It feared the secret and potential dangers of mystery cults and midnight rituals. In 186 BC such fears appeared to have been realised.

▲ *This fresco from the Villa of the Mysteries in Pompeii shows initiation into a mystery cult, perhaps that of Bacchus. The problem for scholars is that we know little of what went on in such cults — and the artist just might have been in the same position.*

Many Romans, mostly women, had been drawn to the Greek cult of Bacchus. This cult was a Greek "mystery cult" where initiates worshipped Bacchus in secret ceremonies, allegedly containing mystical madness, frenzy and uncontrolled sexual misconduct. Stories of Bacchic worship lost nothing in the telling and the state took measures to stamp out the cult. There remained within the Roman psyche a deep mistrust of anything unregulated, particularly if women were involved, and later scandals received similar repressive treatment.

🔲 *Vestal Virgins* 🔲

The single most important priestly office for women was the college of the Vestal Virgins, six highly born women who entered the service of the goddess Vesta, guardian of the sacred flame which signified the hearth (in Latin, *focus*) of the community, at the age of six. They served the goddess for thirty years after which they could marry if they wished, but the Romans thought such a marriage unlucky.

Their privileges were many: they were released from the legal power of their father (though they came under the eye of the *pontifex maximus*); they were not required to have a *tutor* and could make wills and transact business. They had special seats of honour at Roman festivals, including the Arena. However, the penalty for breaking their vow of virginity while in the goddess's service was terrible. A transgressing Vestal would be buried alive by a special ritual and her lover executed.

◄ *The Vestal Virgins lived in Rome near the house of the* pontifex maximus. *The remains of their house may still be seen. Statues of chief Vestals decorate their quiet garden.*

🔲 *Women and Work* 🔲

Women in Roman society undertook a variety of professions if they had to work for their living. We know very little of the actual daily lives of lower class and slave women but their epitaphs and other records reveal the types of jobs they did and the businesses they undertook.

A woman could change her social status depending on how successful she was in her profession. Women were nurses and midwives, dressmakers and hairdressers. They could and did run their own businesses, own their own slaves, and become patrons to local communities. Some women ran taverns, some ran brickworks. Others managed a flourishing sex industry, for Roman society did not expect fidelity in its husbands — although women employed in this industry were less inclined to publicise it on tombstones or other inscriptions. One rare tombstone boasted that the commemorated "madam" "made her money without defrauding anyone".

Female slaves were at the disposal of their owners. It was not uncommon for women who ran the brothels to raise unwanted baby girls to ensure a supply of younger workers to keep them in their old age! Prostitutes had their own religious cults, and so long as they were

◄ *Many women contributed to the economic life of their towns by running shops and stalls. This relief from Ostia at the mouth of the Tiber shows a vegetable seller.*

▲ *A second woman from Ostia also has a market stall selling, poultry and other foodstuffs. Two monkeys attract and entertain customers while they wait to be served. The hutches at the base contain live rabbits. The basket on it holds live snails.*

registered with the *urban praetor* (city magistrate) could practise their trade legally. They were hardly considered the best elements in society and could suffer at the hands of the law, but at least many women in the industry had the chance to control the income they earned.

Other jobs for women included those of washerwomen, net makers, dye makers, producers of perfumes, vegetable sellers and that most significant of all duties for women in the ancient world, weavers and wool workers. These "respectable" jobs were a source of pride to those who performed them and were often recorded in funeral commemorations.

▶ *One's employment was often portrayed on a funeral monument, regardless of gender. A midwife from Ostia is commemorated performing the central task of her profession — assisting at childbirth.*

61

⊠ *Empresses of a Proud Empire* ⊠

Even though the Romans had a fear of powerful women, the concentration of power in one household made it inevitable that certain women from the Imperial House would dominate the political imagination.

Livia and Octavia, the wife and sister of Rome's first emperor, Augustus, started this tradition. Augustus' granddaughter Agrippina, proud of her "royal" blood and conscious of her children's right to power, was darling of the Roman army. Her daughter, also Agrippina, placed her son Nero in control and virtually ruled jointly until he murdered her. Mothers, wives and sisters of later emperors carried on this tradition: Plotina and Matidia, wife and sister of the emperor Trajan, both figured prominently in his reign. Hadrian, his successor, gained power first by marrying Matidia's daughter and then through the contrivance of Plotina. Both Livia and Plotina managed to convey the image of loyal wife and faithful adviser, although the historian Tacitus implies that Livia at least was guilty of many crimes.

Throughout many Imperial dynasties in Rome where men failed to have children, the female line was essential in providing likely heirs. The lack of a clear successor, however, made competition fierce and allowed various historians to accuse the women of each family of plotting to put their particular candidate in top place. Daughters could often miss out.

Augustus' only child, Julia, was married to three men important to her father, and had five children to her second husband Marcus Agrippa. As Augustus had no other children, her sons became his hope of a descendant succeeding him. In the years when they were growing up, Julia was crucial to Augustus' ideology and practical policy. After the death of Agrippa, she was married again to Tiberius, Augustus' step-son. The marriage was unhappy and Julia, who reputedly always lived on the edge of being "caught" for her many affairs, was banished for her "debased" lifestyle in 2 BC. Her elder sons died some years later and her estranged husband inherited Augustus' position in 14 AD. Her third son died soon after. No attempt to reinstate her was successful. Julia eventually died in exile.

Did her father simply live too long? Had he died before the disaster, she, as the mother of a successor, could have been Rome's most powerful first lady. Instead, the story of her last years in exile are one of the most tragic in Roman Imperial history.

The Myth of Coriolanus and His Mother

In 509 BC Lucius Junius Brutus led the Romans against the kings and exiled them. The Roman Republic was founded and Rome was governed by elected magistrates, consuls who worked with the Council of the Fathers, the Senate. The energy and skill of this young Republic led it to victory. Their leaders had ready made chances for glory as the State grew. One of the heroes of the State was Gaius Marcius Coriolanus, who defeated the town of Corioli and its people the Volsci in 493 BC. But Rome had an internal problem. In the first years of the Republic, the Patricians were a separate caste. They controlled the magistracies, the priesthoods and the armies. The Plebeians, (the rest of the people) were fighting hard to gain rights for themselves.

Coriolanus was a proud Patrician. He treated the Tribunes of the Plebs with disdain which led to a fight. When he was charged, he refused to appear in court and was exiled in his absence. Filled with bitterness, he went to his enemies the Volsci and offered to lead them against Rome.

Coriolanus and the Volsci now defeated the Roman armies sent against them. They camped five miles from the city walls and prepared to attack. The Senate and people panicked. They sent ambassadors and priests begging Coriolanus not to destroy them but he refused to listen.

When all else failed, the women of the city turned to Coriolanus' mother, Veturia. Although she knew her son would be destroyed if she intervened, she went to him and called upon him to remember what would happen to them if the Volsci triumphed. She reminded him that he was a Roman, whatever he had suffered. Coriolanus could not ignore his mother. He gave his word he would not fight and persuaded the Volsci to withdraw their army. Veturia and her companions returned to Rome. Coriolanus died in exile. As a mother, Veturia grieved for her son but she put the State first. She was remembered in Roman legend as an example of a great Roman Matrona.

Perils Of City Life

▨ Urbs Roma — *the City of Rome* ▨

By the beginning of the first century BC, Rome was a city of perhaps 600 000 inhabitants. By the end of that century, despite suffering civil war, economic hardship and social turmoil, Rome's population was about one million. It was the largest city in the Ancient Mediterranean World and was hardly matched during the European Middle Ages.

How did this mass of humanity survive? Most of it was crowded into shaky tenement buildings, dependent not only on the state subsidies (granted only to citizens) but on private patronage and special associations. Even the rich were not immune from epidemics and food shortages.

Feeding and providing water and sanitation for this huge metropolis took immense organisation and control of the resources of an empire.

◀ *Doing the laundry was a complicated business in Rome where togas were 6 metres (20 feet) long. Here two fullers fold the washed clothes waiting for customers to come and collect them.*

▲ *The Tiber River which runs through Rome was originally a source of water but was also a rubbish dump and sewerage outlet. The Romans threw into it the bodies of executed traitors. When the particularly unpopular emperor Tiberius died, the mob yelled "To the Tiber with Tiberius".*

The Cess Pit of Romulus

The late Republican politician Cicero remarked that his idealistic contemporary Marcus Cato the Younger "thought he was living in Plato's (ideal) republic rather than the cess-pit of Romulus". Cicero meant the dirty politics but there is no doubt that there was a lot of real dirt in Rome. Jerry-built tenement buildings became a source of cheap housing and a constant fire hazard. Cicero and his wealthy wife owned some of these — he remarked that even the mice were afraid to live in them.

Although Rome had extensive water and drainage systems, only the influential individuals had utilities connected to their households. Laws were passed forbidding the emptying of household waste into the street, but this still happened.

▲ *Life in a stone mason's shop was tough. These men work at moving and cutting marble for the many public and private works of the city.*

▨ *Danger in the Streets* ▨

There was no street lighting, no fire department, no police force. Important people surrounded themselves in the daytime with crowds of clients, in the evening with a bodyguard. Magistrates had attendants to clear the streets for them and to remove troublemakers. Less important people moved in bands for safety against armed thugs and gangs who might or might not be acting for a political organiser. Most people relied on friends, neighbours and passers-by for assistance in the event of insult, attack, fire or other disaster. This was the down side of being a free people.

▨ *Augustus Takes Control* ▨

When Augustus assumed control of the Roman Empire in 28 BC, he ordered the city into fourteen regions and sought to tie regional and association leaders to himself. He himself took over the role of the Censors, who were responsible for much city organisation, and carefully

▲ *Grave reliefs often showed a person's occupation. Men are engaged in sawing wood and cleaning clothes — by trampling them in a solution based on the bleaching qualities of urine.*

watched the activities of the *aediles*, the magistrates who organised its practical maintenance. He instituted a quasi-police force and fire brigade and made sure the Praetorian Guard, his "bodyguard", was close at hand. Slowly the city took on a physical and social order, although riots and unrest could still emerge — it was desirable to have a few strong neighbours on certain occasions.

◄ *This terracotta sign of a wine merchant's shop in Pompeii shows two men carrying an amphora of wine. There was no need to read with signs like this!*

▲ *Most of the urban population lived in apartment blocks called* insulae. *This is a model of such a block at Ostia, near Rome, called the House of Diana.*

▨ *Housing* ▨

Construction of housing depended upon the resources of the owner. In tenement buildings, the ground floor was safest. It had the closest access to water. The higher one went, the greater the risks from the building falling down or being trapped in a fire. Water and the latrines were a long way from these dwellings. Chamber pots were popular but legal cases could arrive if they were thrown at or emptied on passers-by who could afford litigation.

▨ *Life on the Hill* ▨

Status conscious Romans looked to the exclusive Palatine Hill with its extortionate rents. This was close to the Forum, the centre of political activity in the Republic, and to the Circus Maximus, a major source of entertainment. In the time of the emperors, the Palatine was eaten up by the Imperial residence, thus the hill itself gives us our word for palace.

▲ *Garden painting from the House of Livia at Prima Porta. Elaborate painted decoration was common in the houses of the prosperous in and around Rome.*

Large individual houses, many of which were located on the Palatine or in other fashionable areas, could contain their own baths, heating, and pleasure gardens. The entrance hall (*atrium*) displayed mementos of glorious achievements and the "images" (the wax death masks) of ancestors who had achieved high public office. The atrium of the house was also the centre of activity. Women might weave there, children might play, a patron would receive his clients each morning.

▧ *Rome's Social Life* ▧

Rome was a very social city. There was little privacy in the tenement buildings and even the houses of the well-off had large populations of dependents and slaves in addition to the nuclear family.

People gathered with their social equals in associations (*collegia*) based on kinship, neighbourhood (*vici*), occupation, religious cult, affiliation with a political leader or a chariot team, or support for a particular politician or general. All involved communal festivals, social interaction, and mutual benefits such as paying for members' funerals and assisting their families in times of need.

🔲 *Patrons and Patronage* 🔲

Vertical lines linked the various socio-economic groups to each other. Richer and more prominent citizens acted as patrons either to individuals or to associations. The less powerful, the "clients", attached themselves to these "patrons" and received protection, legal and economic assistance, and advice on a variety of matters (sometimes even suggesting marriage partners for clients' daughters). In return patrons expected the client's allegiance, particularly in Republican times when a citizen's vote counted.

Every morning, clients gathered in their patron's house to greet him and accompany him to the Forum in a large group (thereby affirming his importance). A patron might attend a client's household celebrations such as birthday parties, weddings and especially a son's coming of age. He might provide places at the games and other entertainments, especially if he or an associate were seeking election. He might enrol his clients in his legions or depend on them if he needed a gang of burly bodyguards.

Women, if they were wealthy enough, might also become patrons by bestowing benefits on individuals or groups, by investing money in their businesses, by paying for their funerals. If either men or women freed their slaves, the freedman or woman regarded their former owner as their patron.

In some instances the association between patron and client was close. The mentality of the city-state in which every resident had the chance to know his or her fellows was to some extent preserved, even in the teeming confusion of Imperial Rome.

🔲 *Feeding the City* 🔲

Keeping Rome fed was a full time business for many people. In the ancient world, food shortages were a constant problem as cities battled with uncertain harvests, difficulties of transport (pirates and shipwrecks at sea; bad roads and inefficient transport on land), storage and spoiling.

The rustic ideal of a peasant household feeding itself from its own property was unrealistic for most of Rome's history. Not merely the resources of Italy but those of Sicily, Sardinia, North Africa (in that period a rich producer of grain) and eventually Egypt were claimed as taxes to feed the bottomless pit of Imperial Rome. Not that the citizen population itself always came first. If for some reason Rome had an extraordinary number of men under arms, the legions were fed and those in the city had to battle with speculators and shortages.

Food riots were an ugly and not uncommon occurrence, and politicians who were popular at other times might then be reviled and even stoned.

A Roman's Diet

The diet for an average Roman (as opposed to the very wealthy who could command very different resources) was basic. Market gardens around Rome grew and sold vegetables and fruit in season. This supplemented the age-old Italian tradition of the kitchen garden which continued to exist wherever a patch of earth made it possible.

Fish was usually available in Roman markets and an important source both of everyday food and the all-round seasoner, fish sauce (very like Asian *garum*). Meat was usually equated with the big public festivals when sometimes hundreds of animals would be slaughtered to the glory of the

▼ *This relief found in Germany depicts a bakery. Bread could either be sold ready made or baked from the customer's own dough in the baker's commercial oven.*

71

gods (who got the offal) and to feed the Roman people (who received a portion of the rest usually in accordance with their station or contact).

Grain was a staple, but harder to obtain and then equally difficult to turn into bread. Flour had to be milled, then baked, and not every household had the means to do that.

◻ *Grain — a Political Tool* ◻

In early times, during shortages, milling might be the gift of a generous patron eager to win favour with his clients. Then politicians seeking a wider audience sought to standardise the price of grain by means of subsidies and state controlled granaries. In 58 BC Publius Clodius in his role as tribune passed a law instituting a free grain dole.

All of these measures, and especially the free grain dole, were greeted with howls of protest. However, the belief that the Roman People was entitled to some benefits from its empire became steadily entrenched. Emperors made it their business to supervise grain handouts, thus outdoing both the idea of individual patronage or popular political strategists. The emperor Claudius revamped the harbour at Ostia and offered special deals to grain importers in an effort to ensure adequate food supplies. At the beginning of the 2nd century AD, Trajan instituted schemes for feeding the children of the poor so that their parents would not be forced to abandon them to starvation and slavery.

◻ *Not Enough Food* ◻

Even with state controlled subsidies, getting fed was a hard thing for the majority of the population. Subsidies were only for citizens and even then, not everyone qualified. The subsidies were only for grain and people still had to find other necessary foodstuffs.

Festivals might bring food handouts from emperors or would-be patrons. The thought of luxurious banquets with larks' tongues, roasted oxen and beautiful exotic delicacies, which took hundreds of slaves to prepare, were as much a fantasy to most Romans as they are to us. Porridge made from the seeds of edible plants like peas, beans and lentils, fish soup and mediocre wine were far more common to the stomachs of most Romans.

▩ *Literacy* ▩

From the evidence of surviving graffiti and widespread references to reading in all kinds of public contexts, scholars believe that many ordinary people could read. Elementary "schools" of a sort for poorer children could be set up by anyone claiming to be a teacher — under shop awnings, in a spare room, or in any available space. Boys and even girls of all social status had a chance in these centres to learn the rudimentary skills of reading and sometimes writing.

Such schooling finished around the age of twelve and those who could afford it went on to higher things, such as reading "the Classics" and learning Greek. Only the children of the rich completed their education by studying law, oratory and philosophy, usually within the confines of

▲ *Relief from a sarcophagus showing a scholar surrounded by his students. These include both men and women. They read and contemplate a* volumen *— a book in the form of a scroll.*

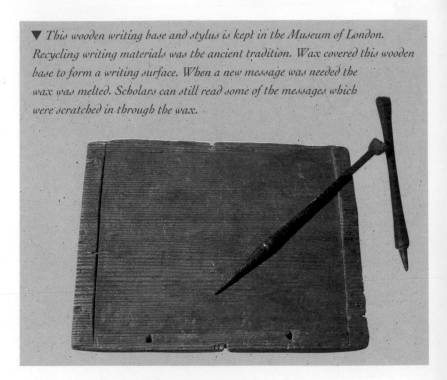

▼ *This wooden writing base and stylus is kept in the Museum of London. Recycling writing materials was the ancient tradition. Wax covered this wooden base to form a writing surface. When a new message was needed the wax was melted. Scholars can still read some of the messages which were scratched in through the wax.*

their own houses or in the homes of distinguished family friends, before taking a trip to the centres of culture in Greece. A female had a good chance of learning to read. Her access to "secondary" education depended on the attitude as well as the resources of her father or husband.

▣ *Posters, Placards and Graffiti* ▣

For advertising and distribution of information, the population of Rome relied on a combination of placards, posters and heralds.

Laws and state business were posted in the Forum. Inscriptions were a common form of commemoration. Graffiti was a popular way of disparaging politicians. Not only Rome but also centres such as Pompeii and Ostia reveal extensive amounts of graffiti praising lovers or even advertising business. Statements like "The thieves and cutthroats support X" were common at election time, probably placed in public view by "X's" opposition. Passers by were even warned to

▲ *Mosaics such as this one from the doorway of a house in Pompeii were designed to discourage intruders. Some were also accompanied by inscriptions like "cave canem" (beware the dog).*

"beware the dog" though the words are accompanied by a picture of a chained watchdog in case they were slow to get the message.

Organisers would advertise games and events by way of posters and banners as well as public announcements. Many individual stunts were explained by placards. Similarly, a general's triumph, a huge victory procession through the Via Sacra which led up to the temple of Capitoline Jupiter, would include placards advertising the places and people he had conquered while floats would commemorate significant events in his campaign. The visual and literary went hand in hand.

Romans might not have been able to read much and possibly could write very little but they often had access to the basic skills of communication.

▲ *Caldarium (hot bath) in the Forum Baths complex in Pompeii. The water was heated by a hypercaust system under the floor. The walls were double-skinned to enable hot air to pass between the two layers and the ceiling was grooved so that the condensed water could drip down the walls.*

▩ *Public Amenities* ▩

The original city of Rome comprised the area of the Palatine and Capitoline Hills and the swampy, mosquito infested marsh in between which became the Roman Forum. Later scholars such as Cicero praised the benefits of the site, and the historian Livy, writing under Augustus, depicts the early Romans debating whether to leave then deciding that their city was too sacred to abandon. But these men were part of the class which could and did abandon this sacred site every summer when their country villas or the seaside towns of the Bay of Naples became infinitely more attractive.

▲ *This aqueduct now known as the Pont-du-Gard, built by Marcus Agrippa in 19 BC, was built to supply water to the colony of Nemausus (modern Nîmes) in the south of France. It is a most famous symbol of Roman culture and engineering in Europe.*

Hills mean valleys and valleys need drainage. The Romans became experts at drains, sewers and aqueducts for getting waste out and fresh water in. They learned their engineering from the Etruscans and taught it to the Romanised world. Reclaiming the land, first in Rome, then in Italy and finally wherever they needed it, became common. The discovery and improvement of Roman concrete and other building techniques allowed them to build down into the sea, to create harbours, breakwaters (such as at Ostia at the mouth of the Tiber river), roads and bridges which still attest their genius for building.

As the city grew rich and men made their mark either by building temples to the gods, or theatres, aqueducts or public baths for the

▲ *Public latrine at Ostia — ablutions were a communal affair. Running water was provided by sophisticated drainage systems both to remove waste and for cleaning.*

people, Rome became an exciting place. The Circus Maximus and the Circus Flaminius hosted chariot races; the public baths allowed both men and women to wash and collect the latest gossip. Markets spread throughout the city. Emperors built lavishly and often encouraged other rich men to follow their lead: forums, porticos, shopping centres, basilicas, baths, temples and theatres sprang up. Public toilets were common, or for quicker and simpler relief for males at least, advantage could be taken of the many receptacles placed in convenient places by the fullers (launderers) who used urine as a natural bleach to whiten clothes. Cook shops, vegetable stalls, garden restaurants added to the attraction of the city. Throughout the Roman world these "civilised" habits were copied on as large a scale as individual cities could manage.

▦ *Spectacles* ▦

A warm climate and overcrowded housing enhanced the Mediterranean attitude of being outdoors whenever possible. People took advantage of the daylight. Work, if one had it, was done early and finished early. The day was free for any of the activities which always drew large crowds.

Law cases were mostly heard out of doors and a popular orator could draw a large crowd. Religious festivals usually implied free food and a good show, sometimes games, races or drama. Public funerals involved processions, banquets and possibly games. When an important public official returned, the people of Rome walked out to greet him. Best of all for a general was the reward of a triumph when he became the city's hero for a day. Riding in a chariot with his face painted red, wearing specially embroidered clothes and a laurel wreath, the triumphing general would conduct the procession. His sons, his soldiers, his supporters, his booty, his important prisoners would all be on display. The people would turn out for the spectacle, largesse and the ensuing feast. They and the general had their feelings of superiority reinforced: he in his achievements, they in the fact that this was another sign of the "greaterness" of the Roman People. Who would have minded the possibility of being mugged on the way home?

High Society on the Bay of Naples

A Greek Settlement

To the south of Rome lay Greek Campania. Stretching out around the Bay of Naples and the surrounding coastline were numerous towns all descendent from the Greeks who colonised the area from the eighth century BC. The Greeks became aware of the trading, mining and farming potential of this area very early.

80

They settled the island of Ischia, then the mainland at Cumae. Other towns ringed the coast. Misenum on the Cape at one end of the Bay, Bauli, Baiae, Puteoli, Neapolis or New City. Down the coast were Herculaneum and Pompeii at the base of Mt Vesuvius. Further to the south were Stabiae and Surrentum. Around the cape from Surrentum was the magnificent Amalfi coast, host to other towns. Inland to the north, and commanding the rich plains of Campania, was Capua.

Rome had shared a close association with these towns from very early in its history. Capua, until it sided with the Carthaginian invader

◀ *This is one of the entrance halls* (atria) *at the House of the Faun at Pompeii. This house was one of the oldest and largest in Pompeii. The statue of the Faun (a copy is shown here) dates to the 3rd or 2nd century BC. The Romans valued antiques as much as we do today.*

▼ *This sacral idyllic landscape is now in the National Museum in Naples. The discovery of such paintings stimulated an interest in the classical world so that the romantic past became high fashion in Europe in the 18th century.*

▲ *The cave of the Sibyl of Cumae was an important part of Roman myth. Virgil, in Book 6 of the* Aeneid *graphically describes the visit of Aeneas, Rome's founder hero, to the gloomy world of the prophetess.*

Hannibal, was so close that the two cities had almost interchangeable citizenship. Rome's first great road, the Via Appia, built in 312 BC linked Rome and Capua. Most towns were linked by special favourable treaties to Rome. The Neapolitans and people of Herculaneum had such a satisfactory arrangement that they took a long time to decide whether or not to give it up in favour of Roman citizenship in 90 BC.

▨ *Real Places in Myth* ▨

The Bay of Naples and the lands which surround it had rich links to mythology, first Greek and then Roman. Aeneas' landing place in Italy was Cape Misenum, his aged nurse gave her name to the town of Caieta. Inland were the Phlegrian Fields and Lake Avernus, the entrance to the underworld. It was here that Aeneas went to ask the advice of his dead father Anchises about how best to fulfil his destiny in Italy. He had as a guide the Sibyl of Cumae, an old woman skilled in prophecy.

In later generations, the Sibyl appeared in Rome where she offered her nine books of prophecy to the king Tarquinius for an enormous sum. He refused and she burnt three. They were offered for the same price. Tarquinius refused again. She burnt three more and made the same offer. Tarquinius could no longer resist. He paid for three what might have bought nine. The books of the Sibylline prophecy were among the most sacred objects in Rome and a special priestly college was appointed to consult them in times of hardship. The temple of Apollo at Cumae and the Sibyl's cave were sacred places.

❖ *Wealthy Romans on Holiday* ❖

From at least the second century, and increasingly from that time, Romans with the resources to do so bought up land around the Bay of Naples. They used the area to escape from the wheeling and dealing of Roman life. These towns all had a bustling life of their own, but compared with politics in Rome, the relative quiet and the opportunity to regain energy was highly prized. The Bay of Naples offered a chance to world weary politicians to "go native" in the holiday period of the year — to mix with the increasingly popular Greek philosophers, to read Greek literature and wear the more comfortable Greek dress.

▼ *A waterside villa from Stabiae, to the south of Pompeii. This wall painting shows a magnificent dwelling by the sea which takes full advantage of its natural environment. If it reflects a real structure, it would have been a major engineering feat.*

Others had less innocent pleasures in mind. The Bay, and in particular the popular northern end around Misenum and Puteoli with its perfect summer climate, lent itself admirably to beach parties and pleasure expeditions. Baiae especially became a seaside resort, the place where Roman High Society went to be seen when Rome was too hot. A woman could tarnish her reputation merely by owning a villa at Baiae.

The geographer Strabo writing in the time of Augustus describes the Bay of Naples as a continuous town because of the number of villas stretching around the coast. Some wealthy owners had more than one. Cicero had three, which he called his "little properties", the younger Pliny had six. The Imperial family had several, both on the Island of Capri and the mainland. Inscriptions suggest, though cannot prove, that the Villa of Oplontis near Pompeii belonged to Nero's wife Poppaea. Her family might also have owned the so-called "House of the Guilded Cupids" and the "House of Menander" in Pompeii itself.

⬛ *Profitable Real Estate* ⬛

Some villas were built with all the engineering skill the Romans could summon to jut out into the sea or to cut through tunnels. The area remained popular even after some towns were destroyed in the frequent earthquakes and the devastating eruption of Vesuvius in AD 79. These villas rose steeply in price and became ever more amazing. In the turmoil of civil war, however, they were the prizes of whatever side won for they were confiscated from the losers and sold at "auction". The dictator Sulla retired to the Bay in about 79 BC, happy to write his memoirs and live a life of quiet opulence. His daughter was just one of the major profiteers in the upheavals accompanying his victory. She bought the villa of Sulla's enemy Marius for 75 000 drachmas (the currency of the Greeks) and sold it not long afterwards for 2 500 000 drachmas, a very tidy profit indeed.

Other villas were not just for pleasure. Run by large slave populations they produced harvests of grain or wine. Those which controlled lakes produced oysters and other seafood. The rich prosperity of Campania made production very lucrative. In Imperial times, the Emperors and their families held huge amounts of land in this area and controlled the large incomes which accrued from them.

◀ *The garden of the so-called House of Octavius Quartio. This serene space had many fountains and nymphaea (grottoes). The water was collected in the roofless* atrium *and stored for use throughout the house and garden both for its aesthetic and cooling properties. The channels were painted blue with decorations of fish and other sea creatures.*

▶ *This wall of a garden in Pompeii shows a garden scene and the shrine of the household gods* (lararium). *The mask above the painting is a theatre mask, a common garden decoration.*

But those who disapproved of the "high life" found much to criticise — extravagance was rife and competition to have the best and biggest continued. Stories of pet fish wearing jewelled collars and granted funerals when they died caused those looking for signs of moral decay to take up their styluses. Petronius' *Satyricon*, a novel written in the age of Nero, describes the sumptuous feast of Trimalchio, a freed slave and now a rich man with an array of delicacies and entertainment. Caligula, in order to outdo the Persian King Xerxes made famous by the Greek writer Herodotus, built a bridge of boats from one end of the bay to the other and rode first his horse and then his chariot across it.

▼ *The House of Neptune and Amphitrite in Herculaneum is called after the mosaic in this open air triclinium (dining room). The triclinium in a Roman house is named for the three-sided arrangement where diners would recline facing the centre to eat their meal. This garden triclinium houses a fountain. Then, as now, the warm summer climate invited outside dinner parties. Houses could have more than one dining area to take advantage of seasonal conditions.*

▓ *Houses of the Rich* ▓

The remains of beautiful villas in Pompeii, Herculaneum, Stabiae and elsewhere attest the comfortable lifestyle of the rich in the Bay of Naples. Houses had not one dining area but perhaps three, one for winter, sheltered from the weather, one for summer, allowing the breezes to cool the diners, and perhaps an outside dining area. The gardens and gracious paintings show a high degree of sophistication. The rich collected antiques from Greece and elsewhere to grace their houses. Paintings of pastoral scenes, of the sea, of mythological scenes, erotic fancy and well-endowed fertility gods graced the walls. Wherever possible, windows opened on to the sea, both to maximise the view and to catch the breeze.

▓ *The Towns* ▓

The towns around these villas thrived as well. From the times of the first emperors Misenum was one of the bases for the Imperial navy. Veterans from various campaigns had been settled around the Campanian countryside from the time of Sulla.

Greek inhabitants and Italian soldiers mixed with all the races of the Mediterranean and created a lively and bustling atmosphere. Traders sold their wares in big markets, cook shops and taverns were numerous. Brothels were marked out by suggestive male genitalia pointing in the required direction. Baths were constructed in the larger of the villa complexes and in the towns themselves for the use of all the townspeople.

These towns had a lively political scene where men vied for local office. Their election graffiti can still be read. In these smaller towns, men who were considered of low status in Rome, such as bakers and fullers (launderers), could become very important in the local town administration. They might also be quite wealthy.

There was much secondary industry. One of these was the production of building materials such as bricks. Men and women both invested in this flourishing industry.

The eruption of Vesuvius in AD 79 destroyed the towns of Pompeii and Herculaneum. But it did not destroy the rich social life of Baiae or the real prosperity of Campania. This continued for as long as the Empire remained.

Roman Emperors — Divine Rulers or Mad?

Some of the most famous Roman emperors are some of the most notorious. The names of Caligula, Nero, Domitian and Commodus are known to many for their excesses, kinky habits or horrible oppression. Caligula was supposed to have murdered both his father and the emperor Tiberius; slept with all his sisters, one of whom he deified before killing; spent every available coin in the treasury on wild living; he even insulted the great Roman army by requesting them

to gather sea shells when they should have been invading Britain. Caligula allegedly made his horse consul because he thought it more intelligent than the average senator.

Tiberius, while not pictured among the truly "mad" emperors, is credited with sexual deviance on the island of Capri by the Imperial biographer Suetonius. Tiberius encouraged informers to gather evidence of treason among senators who subsequently disappeared or were forced to commit suicide. Many of his own family died during his reign.

◾ *Nero* ◾

The tradition of madness continued. Nero, another "bad" emperor, preferred poetry and singing to military achievements and fostered "effeminate" Greek culture over the masculine Roman variety. According to our sources, he was bearable while the senatorial adviser Seneca controlled him, but after he rid himself of both Seneca and his mother Agrippina (whom he murdered after several attempts) he took to the role of tyrant with relish.

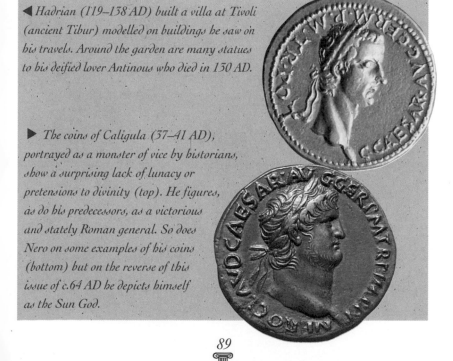

◀ *Hadrian (119–138 AD) built a villa at Tivoli (ancient Tibur) modelled on buildings he saw on his travels. Around the garden are many statues to his deified lover Antinous who died in 130 AD.*

▶ *The coins of Caligula (37–41 AD), portrayed as a monster of vice by historians, show a surprising lack of lunacy or pretensions to divinity (top). He figures, as do his predecessors, as a victorious and stately Roman general. So does Nero on some examples of his coins (bottom) but on the reverse of this issue of c.64 AD he depicts himself as the Sun God.*

89

His sexual "victims" were both male and female. He also indulged in passive homosexuality which, according to Roman moral standards, was far worse than anything else a man could undergo. It was a fact of life for slaves and low born creatures, but no fitting situation for a Roman emperor who was supposed to lead through courage and virility.

Nero mixed a passion for poetry with a desire for divinity, suppression of the Senate, and murder of several people including his wife Octavia. He installed a new and dominating empress, Poppaea, and a nasty "chief of police", the Prefect of the Praetorian Guard, Tigellinus. He sang in public, which was yet another

These two statues show the difference in representations of Roman emperors. On the right is Titus (79–81 AD) in the pose of a senator which stresses his "civilitas", his citizen-like qualities. Claudius (41–54 AD) on the left, is here represented as Jupiter, king of the gods. Claudius was quite amenable to emphasising his close relationship with the gods in official representations. Yet it is his nephew Caligula who is remembered as a would-be god, even though actual iconographical evidence of this desire is hard to find.

source of disgrace. On a tour of Greece, he competed in many events in the Olympic games, all of which he won! Not everyone chose to sit through his long-winded and self-indulgent performances. Some people pretended they were dead.

When a devastating fire broke out in AD 64, Nero was blamed. Rumour spread that he had watched the fire from his palace and sang of the Fall of Troy. He in turn blamed the new secret religious sect of the Christians. Even the historian Tacitus, who did not like Christians, objected to the way Nero had made scapegoats of them.

Domitian

The Julio-Claudian dynasty ended with Nero. The Flavian dynasty took its place. It produced the tyrant Domitian, son of its founder Vespasian. Domitian assumed power in AD 81 and died in 96. His biographer Suetonius tells us that one of his favourite activities was killing flies with a stylus. He describes the battle within Domitian between virtue and vice — vice won. Virtue in fact never had a chance.

Domitian's bad advisers made sure that many senators were accused of treason. Senators in opposition lost their lives, noble women became the object of this emperor's lust and sons of senators were solicited. The regulation list of a tyrant's atrocities continued.

Domitian displayed another striking tendency of a "mad" emperor. He liked chariot racing. Not just watching it but doing it. He also enjoyed grandiose building as had Nero and Caligula before him. Modern Rome still commemorates both these favourite pastimes. The Piazza Navona in Rome is shaped exactly as the building which had preceded it, the Stadium of Domitian.

Commodus

Nero had wanted to rename the city of Rome after himself. So did another "mad" emperor, Commodus, the son of Marcus Aurelius, who died in AD 193. Commodus portrayed himself as the hero Hercules, of whom he was particularly fond. He wiped out most of his family as well as most of the Senate. He even wanted to name all the months of the Roman year after the titles he had given himself.

❖ *A God-Emperor's Fate* ❖

All of these emperors liked to be treated as gods. They took the idea that they were all-powerful to its limits. Most were assassinated either by members of their own court, by senators or by members of their bodyguard. Caligula was murdered by members of the Praetorian Guard in the lunch hour of the Games.

❖ *A Contravention of Roman Tradition* ❖

There is no reason to doubt that power went to the heads of some Roman emperors. But Rome had been founded on the proud tradition of "*Libertas*", freedom. An emperor ruled in direct contravention of this ideal. Much of the tradition of "mad" emperors is bound up with the fact that many Romans had not wanted an emperor and felt that the system of government where one man was in control had

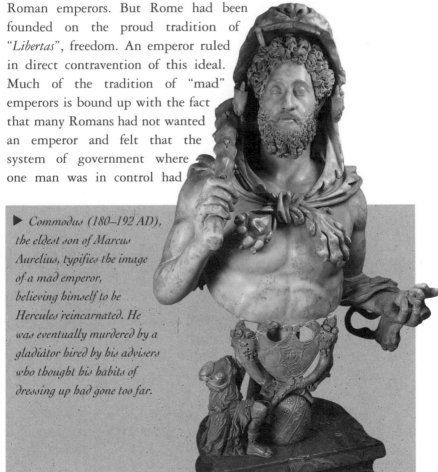

▶ *Commodus (180–192 AD), the eldest son of Marcus Aurelius, typifies the image of a mad emperor, believing himself to be Hercules reincarnated. He was eventually murdered by a gladiator hired by his advisers who thought his habits of dressing up had gone too far.*

been foisted upon them. These men were normally members of the literate and powerful elite classes. As such they suffered the most and wrote the histories.

Emperors like Augustus and Trajan found a balance. They ruled by consent of the governed and particularly of the governing classes. Yet even they were opposed. Others who were remembered well for their achievements were still responsible for the demolition of famous families and important men. Tiberius displayed a genuine interest in having an independent Senate. Yet the four leading senators whom Augustus considered as worthy as Tiberius to be emperors died after his succession. Vespasian emerged as victor in the turmoil following the death of Nero. He fostered an image of being "one of the boys" but when he suffered opposition from the adherents of Stoic philosophy, he wiped them out. Most emperors had to combat competition from within their own families as well. Caracalla, an emperor in the early third century, killed his brother Geta. When the Senate deified Geta, Caracalla apparently remarked, "I don't care if he is a god, so long as he's dead".

The emperors classed as mad earned virulent hatred and a damnation of their memory, but all emperors clashed on occasion with others who believed they had a right to share in government.

Augustus — Son of a God

When Augustus assumed sole domination of the Roman state in 28 BC he slowly set up a way for the political classes of Rome to accept him. He fostered the belief, partly true, that they had chosen him to lead them in government. He engendered a spirit of co-operation which would include all elements of society into his orbit. Yet he took on the trappings of the most well-known form of monarchy, the Hellenistic kingships of Egypt, Syria and Macedonia. This happened in part because he ruled those areas of the world and they began to treat him and his family as divine royalty. But this policy was more than allowing the peoples of the East to treat him as they would their own rulers.

It suited him to deify his adopted father, Julius Caesar, and he took every opportunity to remind onlookers that he was the son of a god. He had every expectation that he would be named a god after his death. In

▶ *The Gemma Augusta dates to c.10 AD and shows Augustus, identified as Jupiter, seated beside the goddess Roma and accompanied by other deities. His rule of the Roman world is made part of the divine order.*

▶ *The Grand Cameo of France shows Tiberius seated with his mother Livia and surrounded by various members of the Imperial House. Augustus, now a god, watches benignly from above. Various "barbarian" conquered people watch from below. The two cameos stress the increasing trend to deify members of the Imperial House as a mechanism of control and power.*

Rome's provinces, temples were founded to "Rome and Augustus". In Italy, his "genius" or engendering spirit, was venerated. He was made sacred by vows of allegiance and by the prayers for his safety that were made throughout Italy.

Even his name, Augustus, a title created for him in 28 BC, implied a closeness with the gods. When he died, he was worshipped and temples sprang up to him around the Roman world.

🔹 *The Emperor's Family* 🔹

Divinity not only attached to the emperor. His family was honoured. Livia, wife of Augustus and mother of his eventual successor, Tiberius, was named Mother of the World in provincial inscriptions. The belief that the emperor and his family were sacred tied people to them and to Rome both in Italy and throughout the Empire. Part of the success of the Julio-Claudian dynasty lay in the successful policy begun by Augustus that the family was descended from the gods and that divinity was still in them. Claudius, Livia, Vespasian, Titus, Trajan, Trajan's wife Plotina, Hadrian and others were all deified.

🔹 *"Good" or "Bad" Emperors* 🔹

The difference between the "good" and "bad" emperors is that the good were rewarded after their deaths by others with the title of "god", the bad assumed it for themselves. The good somehow worked to achieve a balance in dealing with the sensibilities of the elite of Rome. The bad played the tyrant, or at least allowed other interests to override the need for the lasting good opinion of Rome's literate classes.

◄ *Marble relief showing a lararium — formerly household gods but here members of the Imperial family. Augustus is in the centre. He holds the symbols of an augur and his head is covered in the manner of a pontifex. Beside him are one of his grandsons and a figure who is perhaps his daughter, Julia. By identifying themselves with the household gods the Imperial family became part of the daily ritual of many families.*

▲ *Women as well as men were commemorated in some Imperial coinage. Here Agrippina II, great granddaughter of Augustus, shares space with her husband Claudius in a coin from c. 50 AD. She has the title Augusta, which we might translate as "Empress", but for the Romans the word had religious as well as political associations. On the gold coin on the right from 296 AD, Constantius I wears Hercules' lion skin. By 296, Hercules had become part of the official ideology, with two senior emperors calling themselves Jupiter and two junior emperors called Hercules. Constantius I, father of Constantine the Great, was part of this tetrarchy (rule of four co-emperors).*

Efforts are made by scholars to rescue the reputations of emperors damned by their contemporaries. Some efforts are more credible than others. But the idea that the emperor was divine and above the common run of mankind took root and grew. It became a cornerstone of the stability of the Roman World.

Games, Gladiators and Circuses

▩ Roman Holidays ▩

The idea of holidays and festivals was an essential part of the life of any Mediterranean city state. These holidays were associated with worshipping the gods but they also took the place of a modern society's weekend. In Rome, holidays were a time when the State undertook to provide entertainments both to honour the gods and bring pleasure to the people.

🔲 *Etruscan Beginnings* 🔲

The Etruscans, whose kings dominated Rome for at least three generations, were fond of such activities as wrestling and chariot racing, acrobatics, and fights between wild beasts. Their towns were built around a large area set aside for the whole population to enjoy the sights.

The Etruscans appeared to have practised human sacrifice. Prisoners of war were put to death, sometimes by mass stoning. This occurred not only as part of ritual worship, but as funeral games for dead aristocrats. This ritual killing developed into organised combat, the prototype of the gladiatorial arena. The Etruscans also held fights between men and bulls, the foundation of modern bull fighting. These spectacles were very popular.

🔲 *Greek Influence* 🔲

Rome came heavily under the cultural influences of the Greeks. The literate and educated classes enjoyed the philosophy, literature and art of Classical Greek city-states. However when it came to festivals, most Romans preferred the blood sports of the Etruscans. Greek comedy and tragedy was brought to Rome but never really became popular.

Central to such festivals as the Olympic games was the concept of the aristocratic athlete, a person who would make his body as perfect as possible, because he had the time to do so, and who would compete to be judged the best. The Romans regarded athletics as morally debilitating and demeaning. For them, nakedness was a sign of low status, not high, and for the most part the upper classes of Rome preferred to watch others compete rather than do so themselves. Greek games remained popular with "Hellenisers" but not with the bulk of the population.

◀ *This Roman copy of a Greek relief shows Menander, a 4th-century Athenian playwright who developed New Comedy as a genre. Decorations inspired by the theatre were popular, especially the masks by which a character was recognised, even though the Romans were nowhere near as enthusiastic about attending plays as they were about more violent pastimes.*

▼ *Mosaic from Piazza Armarina in Sicily depicting the hunting and transporting of wild beasts. The hunts were nearly as exciting as the games themselves. Hunting and transporting the animals involved a huge industry and specialisation of skills.*

🔲 Ludi — *the Roman Games* 🔲

The entertainments provided by the State were called *Ludi* (games). Public business stopped while magistrates, senators, the Equestrian Order, priests, priestesses and the people assembled to watch them. Before the time of the emperors, certain magistracies, especially the *aediles* (the magistrate in charge of the city), supervised the *Ludi*. Young up and coming politicians would borrow massive amounts of money to pay for them in a bid to win popularity.

There were three types of *Ludi*, the *Ludi Circenses* (chariot racing at the Circus), the *Ludi Scaenici* (theatrical performances) and *Venationes* (hunts). The hunts incorporated displays of and fights against wild beasts. The theatre included both Greek style drama and the far more popular mimes, pantomimes and grotesque ballets. The Circus was the most popular.

In early Imperial times, Rome's first race course, the Circus Maximus was enlarged to hold 200 000 people. There were other circuits as well.

▼ *In this terracotta relief (1st century AD) from Campania we see gladiators struggle with wild beasts in the arena. The important spectators view the battle from a safe distance.*

Chariots raced nine times around an elongated track. The seats at the narrow ends were regarded as the best because the spectator had a better chance to watch the all too frequent bloody crashes. Large numbers of tombstones show that the life of a charioteer was short and glorious. Most commemorate young men of between 17 and 25 years of age. Sometimes the race horses were remembered along with them.

The Romans had a sense of the macabre. They also had a delight in violence. Life was cheap and the lives of prisoners of war and slaves were even cheaper than most. However, they also had a respect for courage and military skill. The charioteers of the Roman Circus were heroes while they were successful. But a good stack brought even more joy then that it does among avid racing fans today.

🔲 Munera — *the Gladiatorial Games* 🔲

The disregard for human and animal life was great in the gladiatorial arena. The word *harena* is Latin for sand, sand that was spread to soak up the copious amounts of blood which characterised every aspect of such entertainment. The first of these gladiatorial combats (*munera*) was

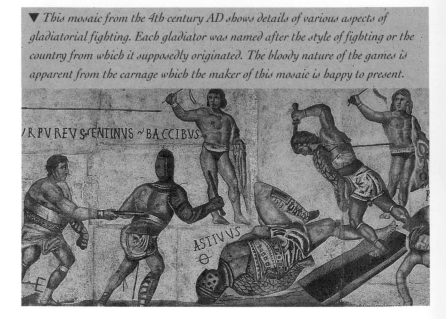

▼ *This mosaic from the 4th century AD shows details of various aspects of gladiatorial fighting. Each gladiator was named after the style of fighting or the country from which it supposedly originated. The bloody nature of the games is apparent from the carnage which the maker of this mosaic is happy to present.*

▼ Boxers were common in ancient Roman games. This mosaic from around the 1st century AD was found in Pompeii. It shows a boxer, his hands bound with protective material. The body got little other protection however, as contests were often carried out by naked competitors.

staged in 264 BC between three pairs of gladiators as part of the funeral of a famous Roman. The idea quickly became popular. Whenever a famous family lost a member, if it could afford the expense, paid for games, particularly if the sons of the family were preparing for election campaigns. Once Rome had an emperor, these *munera* were produced on a massive scale. The emperor paid for most public entertainment, both *Ludi* and *Munera*. He could not really afford to share the popularity it brought with anyone else.

Reflection of Rome's Strength

Both the gladiatorial fights and the wild beast hunts reinforced the idea of Rome's Imperial domination. The military success of Empire provided many prisoners to fight. The poorest citizen could attend the games. He usually sat a long way from the action, but he knew that he was better off than the competitors.

Gladiators were trained in schools and were distinguished by their weapons. Thracians and Samnites were swordsmen, Retiarii were experts with a net and a trident. Others became experts at fighting wild beasts, often deliberately stirring the beasts to the point of madness to keep the fight "interesting". The emperor had to keep a close eye on the training schools for two reasons: Italy's worst slave revolt began when a group of gladiators under Spartacus broke out of a training school in Capua; and individuals who had wanted to control Rome in the political anarchy of the Late Republic owned up to 5 000 gladiators trained as a private army.

Theatrical Blood Sports

Morning was the time for wild beast hunts. The afternoon was for gladiatorial combats. Killing exotic wild beasts in fantasy-inspired scenery or contests between seemingly mismatched pairs was very popular. Dwarfs might fight female "Amazon" warriors, a swordsman might fight a Retiarius and so on. Oddly matched animals were pitched against each other. As ordinary blood-letting became passé, organisers of the games looked for ways to keep people in a state of wonder.

▲ *As well as expensive beast hunts there were cheaper forms of entertainment. This mosaic from the Vesuvius region shows two fighting cocks, another popular sport among the ancient Romans.*

The numbers of animals and people used grew to enormous proportions. Three thousand animals died on the day the emperor Titus opened the Flavian Amphitheatre (better known as the Colosseum). Hundreds of gladiators might fight in the same contest. Lunchtime at the games was used to rid the city of criminals. These were usually untrained and merely thrown to animals. In some of these lunchtimes, Christians were thrown to the beasts.

Executions were regarded as the least imaginative part of the program. Organisers raised interest in them by constructing "scenery" reflecting mythology and legend to bring about the deaths. "Orpheus" might be torn apart by bears when his music failed to soothe a savage beast or two; Daedalus and Icarus might "re-enact" their early flight, with both of them instead of just Icarus falling to their deaths; others might be consumed by fire when dressed in costly garments. Nero turned Christians into human torches in the persecutions following the fire of 64 AD.

Naval fights were mounted as well. An expanse of land was flooded and people gathered to watch a re-enactment of a famous battle. Prisoners or condemned slaves were the sailors. The colosseum could be flooded for such "naumachiae" if the organisers chose.

The Games' Industry

A whole industry arose around the games. Trainers of humans and animals, bandagers, doctors, attendants were among the many. A separate industry developed to hunt and transport animals to Rome. These hunts were themselves a spectacle and a favourite subject for mosaics and paintings. Reserves of game in Africa and Western Asia were seriously depleted, sometimes to the point of extinction in the endless search for the exotic, unusual or popular to "decorate" the Roman Arena.

Heroes of the Games

The gladiators as well as charioteers took on hero status in Rome. They paraded before the games in a manner reminiscent of the triumphant generals of the Republic. Anyone could attend and watch the last meal they took together before the games. Betting on favourites was brisk and popular. Women were reputed to fall in love with gladiators, though it was a permanent slur on any respectable woman's reputation for her to be associated with one. Young men from good families longed to be in the arena fighting as gladiators. Some actually did so though it meant loss of status and disgrace. Some emperors, disregarding the horror of their social peers, occasionally fought as gladiators. They always won.

Spectators out of Control

Controlling a crowd incited by blood proved difficult. In Pompeii, for example, a fight broke out in the crowd between the people of Pompeii and the neighbouring town of Nuceria. The riot grew so large that the participants spilled out of the arena and into the street. The emperor Nero placed a ten year ban on games in Pompeii, a terrible punishment and disgrace for the townspeople. We are told of the fight by the historian Tacitus, but the subject made such an impression that it became the subject for a wall painting as well.

▲ *This painting shows the amphitheatre at Pompeii. The occasion, related by Tacitus in his histories, was that of a riot in 59 AD between the citizens of Pompeii and neighbouring Nuceria. Nero banned games for 10 years as a punishment.*

▨ *For the Spectator — Horror or Fun?* ▨

No-one seriously questioned the brutality of the games, although some philosophers believed it was bad for the people to have that much fun. The games continued even after Christian emperors ruled in Rome and the East. They spread all over the known Roman world. Any city of size had an amphitheatre, sometimes with a capacity for many more than the city population so that visitors from the neighbouring towns and countryside could attend. Even Greece, the home of noble athletics and aristocratic amateurism, built its share of amphitheatres and took eagerly to blood sports. Troupes of gladiators travelled from town to town.

Such displays were thought of as inferior because the entrepreneur could not afford to have any killed.

Christian writers and intellectuals did view the games with horror. Yet they recognised how attractive they were. St Augustine describes a young man determined to go to the games only so he could criticise them. He left completely addicted.

The modern bull ring is a western descendant of the amphitheatre. Sometimes, as at Arles and Nimes in Southern France, the bull fights are held in the remains of its Roman amphitheatres.

▣ *The Cost of Popularity...* ▣

Games, circuses and displays were as constant a drain on the Imperial Treasury as they were on the wild life of Africa and Asia. Yet the emperor could not afford to cancel them. Emperors who showed disdain for the games and cut back the cost of them quickly became unpopular. Those who attended and enjoyed them maintained a good rapport with their people.

▼ *Funerary relief for a magistrate who was responsible for organising a chariot race in the Circus. It shows the key features of this circus: the four horse chariot, the turning points and the statues which decorate it as well as the speed and excitement of the race.*

108

The Arena and Circus were two of the very few places where people could protest about what they did not like or cheer someone they favoured. Emperors used the games to distribute bounty, such as lottery tickets or food. "Bread and circuses" summarised the people's demands of their emperor, and of these, circuses were more popular. For as long as the Empire could afford them, the blood sports of Rome continued.

▼ *This wall painting from Campania shows Aeneas being treated by a surgeon. Soldiers and gladiators received the most specialised medical treatment. Doctors were in attendance at the games to treat wounded gladiators and often gained their knowledge of medicine and anatomy from the wounds the gladiators received.*

The Carrot and the Stick — a Slave's Life

From the time of its first conquests, Rome had access to a slave population. As her empire grew, so did the number of slaves. When the Romans conquered Greece and the East, they brought back teachers, doctors, shepherds, and thousands of others to serve them. When Caesar conquered Gaul, the slave markets were flooded with defeated peoples. So the pattern was set and continued.

The Need for Slaves in Rome

Although there were distinctions of status and economic well-being in Rome, there was no under class which could serve as a ready supply of coerced labour. A free person was free, even if he was poor. As an alternative, the Roman economy, as with most Mediterranean societies, depended heavily on slaves, especially as it expanded in the second century BC and later. Prisoners of war became slaves; victims of pirate raids suffered similarly. The slave markets of Delos in Greece and other places were often packed full with human merchandise. Once a slave population had been established, the women bore children. They too were slaves, "home-bred", who continued the supply even when foreign conquest slowed.

A Slave's Duties

Slaves carried out an extraordinary array of tasks. Some were obvious. They served in the house as domestic servants; they tilled the soil and herded animals, particularly on the large estates which became popular

110

as wealth increased among the few at the top. Other slaves provided a work force in the factories which produced items such as ceramics, knives, shoes and so on. The unluckiest slaves worked in the mines, a certain death sentence for any condemned to it. Most gladiators were slaves, as were all the attendants at the public arena and at the circus. Many prostitutes were slaves, raised by brothel owners for this purpose, as were attendants at the baths and all public amenities.

Slaves had more surprising functions as well. Much of Roman bureaucracy was performed by educated slaves owned by the State. They ran the Mint under the supervision of a magistrate, administrated the Archives and the Treasury and acted as assistants to magistrates. Similarly, slaves assisted the master and mistress of a household in tasks of administration. They often taught the children as well as any promising slave whom the owner thought worth the investment.

▼ *The clever or stupid slave was a stock figure in Greek and Roman comedy. In this relief from the Vesuvius region a master is about to beat his slave, always depicted by an ugly mask.*

A house might own a slave doctor as well as a group of gladiators to act as a bodyguard. Slaves were trained as copyists and so produced books.

With the change in political system from Republic to Emperor, the emperor's household was used as a base for Imperial administration. The slaves of the emperor were a highly privileged group.

Specialist Slaves

Slaves proliferated within each area as well. A rich household did not just have sufficient slaves to do the work. It was a sign of status to have specialist slaves for every aspect of household management. There was not just one cook, but a pastry cook, a meat specialist and so on. Within the house alone there could be hundreds of slaves each with a special function. Even a relatively poor house might own a few slaves, but such a place could not afford the luxury of specialists.

▼ *This wall painting from Campania is of an elegant dressing room where a slave arranges a girl's hair for a special occasion. Favourite slaves, especially nurses and hairdressers, were often commemorated fondly by their mistresses.*

112

▨ *Owned Body and Soul* ▨

A slave was owned, body and soul. As such a slave could be sold at the whim of the owner. People knew that slaves were human but as they were not morally free to make decisions, they were not complete as human beings. They were often physically deformed through hard work or mistreatment, an abhorrent thing to Roman taste. There was a perception that the slave was a foreigner, an outsider and a threat. The Greek philosopher Aristotle believed that slavery was a natural state for some races. Cicero described the Jews and Syrians as "nations fit for slavery". Yet both these men were considered enlightened thinkers in their times.

This view of slavery allowed an owner the right to treat a slave exactly as he or she saw fit. If another person injured a slave, the cost for damages went to the owner who had suffered a loss of property, not to the slave. A slave could become the sexual plaything of his or her owner. Part of the cultural disgust at "playing the woman", that is, taking a passive role in homosexual activity, sprang from the fact that this was thought a reasonable way to use one's slaves. Free men were supposed to be "active", no matter what the gender of their partner might be.

▶ *A typical slave in comedy — slaves were always ugly, old and somewhat deformed. The mask emphasised the convention, which reflected the commonly held view that slaves themselves were morally deformed and not quite whole people. Of course many slaves were actually deformed by their conditions of life.*

Owners could decide what punishment a slave might suffer. Some punishments were worse than others. One slave was covered with honey and left out for the ants. Another master fed his erring slaves to flesh-eating fish. Runaway slaves could be sold to the mines where they would quickly die. If a slave killed his or her owner, all the slaves of the household were put to death.

▓ *Ennus and Spartacus — the Slaves Revolt* ▓

In the second century BC Sicily was flooded with massive numbers of slaves who worked as shepherds and farm workers under minimal control but horrible conditions. These people had been born free and knew the difference between slavery and freedom. A Syrian slave Ennus encouraged his fellow Syrians to believe their gods had chosen him to be their leader and that they would overthrow their masters and take over Sicily. The revolt broke out in 139 BC on a huge scale and for

▼ *Funerary relief depicting a prosperous merchant. Slaves were used in shops both as assistants and craft workers. Here the attendants would probably be slaves and the merchant could be a freed slave.*

many years, the slaves managed to cause disruption across Sicily. It was not until 131 that the revolt was finally quashed. Another revolt broke out about twenty years later, also in Sicily, and was quelled with similar difficulty. These revolts did not spread to Italy.

In 73 BC, revolt did break out under the gladiator Spartacus, a Thracian who had come to Rome as a prisoner of war. Spartacus, whose wife also claimed she could communicate with the gods, defeated two consular armies before Marcus Crassus crushed him and his forces in 71 BC.

▼ *The knife seller Cornelius Antimetus was a prosperous freed slave who was proud enough of his trade to depict it on his funeral monument. He also had no problem in revealing his slave origins.*

While Spartacus was on the loose, all Italy dreaded his presence. When he was defeated, 6000 of his troops were crucified along the Appian Way, the major road into Rome from the south.

Such revolts left a deep impression upon the Roman psyche. Rome needed slaves but had to be able to control them. Its armies were needed elsewhere. The city did not want to pour all its energies into controlling slaves when foreign lands were there to conquer.

Controlling the Slaves

How to achieve a social framework in which slaves were controlled but useful? Many centuries of experience went into answering this question. On the one hand, slave owners became more experienced at owning slaves. Slaves were prevented from forming groups with strong common identity. For example, slaves of the same race, inclination, religious or cultic experience were separated. By law, a slave had no family or kin grouping. His only social unit was his master's house. Most were treated badly but not so terribly they felt they had nothing to lose by revolt. Slave owners united regularly to ensure the return of a renegade or the defeat of a group.

Such measures could only go so far. More effective were the means by which Roman society encouraged slaves to accept their lot. This was done in several ways and over hundreds of years. First and foremost was the hope of honourable manumission, that is, a grant of freedom. Owners freed slaves who had pleased them, sometimes in their hundreds. A freed slave became a citizen and within a generation the descendants of slaves enjoyed the full privileges of citizens of free birth. While a slave believed there was a chance of legitimate freedom, he or she was less likely to run away. If slaves were attached to a household they were part of the *familia*, the group which all came under the power of the Father of the Family. Such slaves might be raised alongside the sons of the House and might become fellow workers in the family business. Some slaves were allowed considerable freedom to conduct business as his owner's proxy. In some cases, he was allowed to retain some of the profits and use them to buy himself from his master. Such slaves controlled other slaves, and these people also controlled slaves under them. The slave in this scheme was not an outsider but a part of a community.

The first emperor Augustus paid special attention to slaves and freed slaves in his reconstruction of the Roman state after the civil war period. All the warlords had encouraged runaway slaves to swell the forces of their competing armies. Once in control, Augustus stopped this, returning 20 000 slaves to their owners. He also discouraged mass emancipation by the owners of large households. But he tied loyal slaves in a close bond to himself. Slaves were included in religious festivals and freedmen formed a special priestly college in the Imperial cult, the Augustales. Freedwomen who bore four or more children were released from the need of a male guardian in their business transactions. Other emperors bettered the conditions of slaves. Claudius ruled that an owner had no right to claim back a slave he or she had abandoned when sick.

▼ *This mosaic shows a dining scene with household slaves serving and entertaining guests. Slaves in a rich household had highly specialised tasks. The more the slave's job was demarked, the higher the family's prestige.*

▲ *Relief depicting a foundry with two characters, one of whom could be the master, the other a slave. In small family businesses it was common for slaves and masters to work closely together.*

As foreign conquest happened less, many slaves were "home-bred", that is born of slave parents and raised within the context of a Roman household. They knew no other life but that which their owner ordained for them.

Some Romans freed their slaves and then made them heirs. Many tombstones record the grateful acknowledgment of a freed slave to a patronus or patrona, a male or female former owner. The relationship between former owner and slave was significant. Former slaves were expected to treat former owners with respect. They were meant to leave them a certain amount of property and to work a certain number of days per month in their former owner's service. Freedom came at a price.

A sensible owner allowed slaves to set up a family. Often the owner might require a husband and wife team to run his or her property. An owner could choose the partner for the slave. He or she could terminate the relationship. However, there grew increasingly the belief that such

▲ *This mosaic from Tunisia shows hefty slaves with large jugs of wine serving the enthusiastic drinkers.*

marriages should not be broken wantonly and that slave parents should not be separated from their children too quickly. This contravened the idea that a slave had no independent *familia*, that he or she depended completely on the owner for any "kinship" structure. A freedman might have to find the money to "buy" his wife's freedom. He might then have to find the money to "buy" their children's freedom, because any children born to slaves were the property of their owner. They then had to adopt their own children because by Roman law there was no legal relationship.

If a free man wanted to marry a slave, he first had to free her and then marry her. Women did not usually free their male slaves for this reason without attracting a good deal of social disgrace.

🔲 *The Carrot and the Stick* 🔲

Some of the improvements in the conditions of slavery have been attributed to adherence to the Stoic philosophy which believed in a universal soul of the human race. More often, however, they occurred because it was impossible to control a huge slave population without getting many slaves on side. The carrot was there — the possibility of independent wealth, of freedom, of the opportunity to begin a *familia*; the opportunity to become a member of the slave-owning class.

But the stick remained too — slaves could still be bought and sold, their lives controlled in a way most of modern humanity could not accept. They were denied a personality by law. They could still be brutally mistreated. Wide scale revolt ceased but slaves still ran away and took to the hills.

Most significantly of all, any improvements which occurred coincided with the fact that life was becoming increasingly difficult for free-born people of low status to maintain their privileges. The lines between who was a slave and who was free were blurred. And this was very much to the detriment of the poor and unimportant person, whether he or she was free or a slave.

◄ *This wall painting depicts a dining scene where slaves serve guests at a banquet.*

Death and the Afterlife

"I was not; I was; I am not; I don't care".

This phrase was not uncommon on Roman graves. It summarises the direct antithesis in belief between Romans and Christians who believed that life really began with death, their mode of entry to their Heavenly reward.

The Romans were confronted daily with death. Because of their reasonably healthy diet and climate, some people lived a long time if they survived certain critical periods. However, many children did not live past infancy. Disease or trauma could carry off the very young; childbirth killed many women, and war took a major toll on the men, especially in those periods when Rome was establishing its empire or fighting civil war.

▶ *A Roman sarcophagus from the 2nd century AD — at one end a doorway of a tomb is illustrated along with the various decorations which might be found near a funerary monument.*

Epidemics could kill many thousands of people in a few months. Excavations in Rome in the nineteenth century, for example, revealed mass graves of perhaps 24 000 people. We know that some corpses could have been dumped because city inscriptions ordered people not to do so. One such inscription requesting people to dump bodies and rubbish outside the city was reinforced by the terse graffito: *"Move shit further on if you want to avoid trouble"*.

◀ *This silver cup from Boscoreale, near Pompeii, is decorated with skeletons having a party, reflecting the common Roman attitude of "we'll all be like this when we're dead".*

▼ *A fresco which possibly depicts an antomy lesson. Medical knowledge varied considerably mostly because of the taboos on human dissection which, though practiced in certain periods, was very uncommon.*

Medical Treatment

Medical knowledge existed and was quite extensive but not everyone had access to doctors or chose to consult them. Often a slave had a better chance of treatment if he or she was valuable property to an owner who retained a doctor in his or her household. A soldier might have a better chance of surviving a wound incurred in battle than a free poor man in the streets of Rome because the army had access to doctors. A valuable gladiator might be patched up by the entourage of the person who owned his troupe. The rest of the population managed as best they could and that usually was not very well.

Spirits of the Dead

Such a huge prevalence of death and the sentiment expressed in the simple grave message might suggest an indifference to death. Despite the nihilistic gravestone message, the Romans did care, though they were not always able to do anything about what happened to their mortal remains when they died. Proper burial rituals ensured that the *manes*, the spirits of the dead person, reached the world of the dead safely and did not wander about in an eternal search for a home. No living Roman wanted these manes to be on the loose for such spirits could be angry, or worse still, harnessed by witches to provide power for magical activities. On the other hand, when correctly laid to rest, the *manes* could become part of the protective guardian spirits of the household. The worship of these spirits was part of household religious observance.

Funerals for the Great

The world of the dead was a shadowy vague place where individuals mattered little. It was therefore important that people on earth maintained a clear memory of a person for as long as possible. This earthly commemoration was immortality for a Roman. For those of the upper class, especially men who held public office, a funeral was a grand occasion which reminded the people of the greatness of the individual and the family.

L·VIBIVS·L·F·TRO VECILIA D·L·HILA
L·VIBIVS·FELICIO·F·IX·VILIA·L·L·PRIM

▲ *Funeral relief of the family of Vibius in Rome showing all the traditional characteristics of a sternly moral Roman family. Note the equality in size and prominence of husband and wife and the early death of their son.*

Polybius, a Greek, describes the ceremony as he saw it around the middle of the second century BC. The dead person was carried into the Forum. Others who had achieved public office were represented by actors wearing wax death masks (*imagines*) and wearing the garments which signified at a glance the dignity of each one. A son of the family pronounced the obituary, thus publicly linking himself to the greatness being celebrated. The body of the dead person would be cremated, a huge feast given for the city population, and the remains deposited, often in an ostentatious tomb. The death mask would then join the others in the family atrium, the main room of the house. Nothing could be more inspiring, Polybius says, to an ambitious young man than the glory given to the illustrious dead.

▲ *The tomb of the Haterii showing the laying out of a body and funerary rites in the presence of mourners.*

▨ *Other Funerals* ▨

Only the families of great public figures had access to such magnificent display. Others, however, settled for less. A *familia* in Roman culture included the *paterfamilias*, the father of the household, his children, his slaves, his freedmen and freedwomen and others who might have been attached by kinship or association. A good *paterfamilias* was responsible for the health and welfare of all his household, and thus would provide medical help for the sick and burial for the dead. The ashes of all family members, sometimes including slaves, would be deposited in mausoleums which might or might not commemorate individuals. On occasion, a childless person might adopt his or her freedmen and women as heirs. They would eventually be buried along with their former owners. The rituals for the dead applied to the whole *familia*.

◀ *Groups of family tombs were modelled on dove-cotes or columbaria. In a columbarium, ashes of the dead were housed in jars set into small niches. Fashions of either cremation or inhumation prevailed at different periods in Roman history.*

Burial Fraternities

Those who did not belong to a great household or who were not wealthy in their own right were harder pressed to arrange a proper funeral. Many formed burial fraternities. Contributions to this fraternity would eventually pay for the burial of the person and his family.

These associations were social as well. Members of a burial club met for a sacred meal on appointed days of the year and feasted lavishly. Often this feast was in the mausoleum of the club among the remains of their dead associates. Free and slave joined these associations. The entry fee for a burial club at Lanuvium in Italy in the middle second century AD was 100 sestertii (not a large sum) and an amphora (jar) of "good wine" and a low monthly fee. In this club, there were at least six feasts for the living per year. This club also had a patron who provided funds for a feast on the festival days of the club's patron gods. If a slave member was freed, he was expected to provide an amphora of wine for his associates.

The Roman government did not like any associations because they were thought to encourage deviant political discussions. Burial associations were permitted because they served a fundamental cultural need but the law restricted their meetings to once a month and the exact purpose of the club had to be clearly reiterated at each meeting.

▶. *"Death the great leveller" — death was all around the Romans, even on the dining table. This mosaic from Pompeii depicts a skull crowned with a level with a plumb line hanging from it.*

▩ *Freed Slaves* ▩

Some freed slaves who became wealthy were anxious to show their status to the world. They were particularly anxious to demonstrate that they were the founders of a new *familia*. Husbands and wives might be portrayed on tombstones along with reference to their successful professional lives. Young children, even those of slaves, were frequently commemorated by simple inscriptions. Although we cannot really recover any real sentiment from the formulaic commemorations, the quantities of funerary inscriptions to all strata of society attest the importance of being remembered and of paying honour to the dead whenever possible. They also allow us an insight into the ideals of the people who commissioned them even if in some cases the truth was very different.

Popular on commemorations between husbands and wives was the proud boast that they lived together without any quarrel, that they were "most loving" or that they "deserved well". Such protestations were so common that they, like so much else on a stone carving, could be abbreviated. Some people wrote and set up the inscription before they actually died so that its inscription and appearance were what they wanted.

127

▲ *The sarcophagus (stone coffin) could show scenes from the life of the person buried in it. This sarcophagus belonged to a cobbler who is pictured plying his craft.*

🔲 *A Proliferation of Tombs* 🔲

Tombs lined the streets of most Roman cities. Many of Rome's largest monuments are found on the Via Appia and can still be seen alongside the cobbled road. One ostentatious man, Cestius, had a huge pyramid built in the late first century BC at the Ostian gate in Rome. Nothing else about him is known to us except for the commemoration of his career inscribed on

◄ *Funerary monument of P. Vitellius Successus and his wife. The whole family could be commemorated together on such elaborate funeral monuments.*

the tomb. St Peter's Basilica is built on the remains of an ancient graveyard and many of the tombs have recently been excavated. The centre of the Catholic religion was built there because of the belief that it was the final resting place of the remains of St Peter.

▨ *Sarcophagi* ▨

Cremation had always been the preferred means of disposing of a dead body. From the middle second century AD, however, the fashion swung towards inhumation. The body was put in the ground in a coffin which reflected the means of the owner. Stone, wood, lead or a covering of tiles have all been found. The wealthy constructed beautiful sarcophagi which had room for a handsome inscription. The best of these were imported from Greece or Asia Minor. Sarcophagi were quite often recycled (as was everything else of an enduring material in the Ancient World) with very little change to the original structure beyond a new inscription.

▨ *"Eat, drink and be merry, for tomorrow we die"* ▨

The Romans co-existed with death in a way foreign to us. Not only

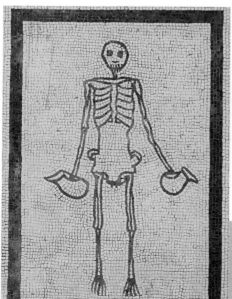

were funeral feasts held inside the burial chamber, but the concept, "Eat, drink and be merry, for tomorrow we die" was commonly expressed in literature and art. Dining rooms featured skeleton-like butlers carrying in the wine, or skulls and other deathly features as patterns for mosaics as the table top.

◀ *This skeleton is called "The Butler" because of the jugs he carries. Associating food with the symbols of death reinforced the ephemeral nature of life.*

In the satirical "Feast of Trimalchio" of Petronius' *Satyricon*, a slave brings a skeleton into the middle of the feast. Trimalchio says: "Man's life, alas, is but a span, so let us live it while we can. We'll be like this when we're dead." He has already planned a tomb to outdo anyone's and has his will read out so that the beneficiaries could thank him while he is alive.

"*Eternal Reward*" — *Other Religions*

The nihilistic concept of the afterlife was unsatisfying to many in the Roman world. The possibilities of what lay beyond life formed the basis for endless speculation and eventually a predilection for all kinds of cults and philosophies, particularly in the East. This was part of the attractiveness of religions such as the worship of Isis and of Mithras and particularly Christianity, all of which had a richly developed sense of eternal reward.

The Catacombs are the most famous Christian tombs in Rome. They were underground burial chambers used mostly between the third and fifth centuries. The inscriptions to Christians are mostly very simple. One interesting development was a tendency to record the date of death as well as the age at death. The date of death in Christian theology was a new birthday into the Life with Christ.

◄ *A mithraeum was a temple to the saviour god Mithras. It was built to resemble a cave. Small groups of men would gather to carry out the rituals of their religion. Such "mystery" religions were popular because they promised eternal life to the initiates.*

▲ *Catacombs were painted undergound tombs for Christians. They are based on the Columbarium style of tomb. Their artwork represents the first truly Christian developments in art and iconography.*

◀ *These are two examples of catacombs of Rome. These underground tombs were burial places for Christians, not places for persecuted Christians to hide as movies suggest. The Christians saw death as the beginning of a new life and recorded the date of death as well as adding their own symbolism to their funerary inscriptions.*

The Coming of Christianity

The world of the Roman Empire was militarily stable. Once Roman domination was complete, there were few challenges to Roman might. This was "the Roman Peace". Within the Roman Empire, cultures, ideas, particularly religious cults, could travel widely. The Emperor of Rome was central, however, to everybody's world. Whatever community you belonged to, whatever gods you worshipped, you worshipped the Emperor and his family as well.

A Flexible Empire

With few exceptions the Romans had a deep regard for the laws and traditions of the peoples they controlled. Wherever it was possible to adapt and accept local custom they did so. Rome itself was a multicultural environment where many foreign communities introduced their own religions without interruption to the pact with the gods of the Roman state. Only when an institution or a person was seen as a threat to Roman power was it or the person removed. The Druids of Britain were driven into the sea because they were seen as chief agents of revolt; Jerusalem was destroyed after a rebellion many years in the making. Such projects were costly and relatively rare. For the most part, Rome ruled by the consent, however grudging, of the Empire.

Why then is the Roman Empire known to many people today as that monstrosity which was responsible for religious persecution, in particular, persecution of Christians? General ignorance and fear of what was different was the first problem. Insecurity of those in power the second.

▩ *First Christian Scapegoats* ▩

"Christians" was a term first used in the Syrian city of Antioch to abuse the followers of Jesus of Nazareth. For the Romans, Judaea had been a troublesome area for some years. Jesus was probably seen as just one more troublemaker, that is, if they gave the matter any thought at all. Some Christians moved to Rome and lived within the Jewish communities which lived a precarious existence in the Transtiber region of the city.

When the fire of Rome burnt most of the city in AD 64, the emperor Nero needed scapegoats. He first chose the Jews. They escaped on this occasion because his wife Poppaea Sabina had an interest in their learning. According to Tacitus, who wrote in the early second century AD, Nero turned on the Christians, a detested sect because of "their hatred of the human race".

This was the first clash between Rome and the new religion. Tacitus' contemporary Pliny gives us information on another in his letters to the emperor Trajan when he governed the eastern province of Bithynia. Christianity had grown in numbers and had been brought to the governor's attention. Pliny was at a loss to know how to deal with them. He knew it was a crime to be a Christian but did not know why. Wild stories about their practices had spread, including charges of cannibalism, incest and orgies, but Pliny, after torturing some Christians for evidence, refused to believe this. However, he saw this "depraved and excessive superstition" as a threat to Rome because of the secrecy and exclusivity of their meetings and their obstinacy. He told Trajan that he had induced many to reform their ways but did not know what to do with other reprobates. Should he seek them out? Trajan gave a reply which seemed reasonable to him and Pliny, but which later Christian writers regarded as infamous. He commended the course of action taken by Pliny and said that Christians should be punished, but they should neither be sought out nor should any notice be taken of anonymous information. There was to be no witch hunt.

Later that century when Marcus Aurelius was emperor trouble broke out in the important Gallic city of Lugdunum (Lyons). The people rioted against the new "Greek" sect of Christians. Hundreds of Christians, according to the accounts of Christian authors, suffered an ugly death in the Arena. The emperor Marcus Aurelius later approved the punishments, but the act was neither begun nor directed by him. Popular hatred and mistrust lay behind the desire to eradicate this new "foreign" religion. In Marcus' only comment upon the Christians he too stated that they were obstinate.

▼ *This wall painting from Herculaneum depicts a ceremony at a temple of Isis. Isis, the mother goddess, was a popular figure of worship. Her rites were tolerated by the Roman government but under careful control. Isis worship had a profound salvation/immortality message, which contributed much to Christian thought.*

▲ *Wall painting from the House of the Physician in Pompeii. Its subject matter is the judgement of Solomon. This painting is often cited as evidence of a Jewish presence in Campania in the 1st century AD and the general knowledge of Jewish literature.*

▨ *Why Were People Against the Christians?* ▨

It is important to note that the first persecutions were not begun because of official policy. Even Nero was looking for a way out of a potentially nasty situation rather than eradicating a threat. It was popular hatred which made the Christians vulnerable. Official attention came second.

This lack of tolerance is all the more surprising in the context of the second century AD. Interest in religion was very strong in this period, particularly in the East where oracles and prophetic cults had a large popular following. Marcus Aurelius himself had an interest in the human-headed snake oracle, Glycon of Abonouteichos, and its prophet, Alexander, spurned by the contemporary satirist Lucian as an egregious fake. Wandering philosophers and teachers attracted followers and people turned with new energy to the Schools of Plato, Aristotle, Epicurus and the Stoa. People joined the "mystery cults" in large numbers and worshipped in secret ceremonies such gods as Isis, the

great mother, and Mithras, the saviour god of the East. Such religions promised a rich afterlife and eternal happiness which the traditional community religions of the Greek and Roman world failed to do.

Traditional community religion did not exist for the good of the individual. It protected the community of which everyone was a part. The pact with the gods did not call for ethics. It called for observance of ritual and honour to the deities which underpinned a state's prosperity. To ignore them was to shatter the *pax deorum* (peace treaty with the gods). In every other case, a person with a devotion to a personal religion kept alongside it the ancestral observance of his or her community. In this way no god could be offended and therefore made angry.

In the eyes of people around them, Christians were arrogant, separatist and anti-social. They would not join in the community holidays and celebrations which were all devoted to the community's gods. They could not become state magistrates because such officials had to pray for the community to the gods. They should not have (but probably did) become soldiers in the Roman army. Worse still, the early Christians imminently expected the end of the world and believed that all but they would be consumed by fire and damnation. The community knew nothing of the philosophy and saw only the hostility to them and their traditional way of life. To them, the Christians "hated the human race".

▩ *"Weird" Beliefs of the Christians* ▩

Stories grew up accusing this "weirdo" sect of cannibalism and incest. Killing babies was another favourite charge. The ancients had a strong sense of magic and witchcraft and assumed that Christians were involved in these anti-social practices as well. They were thought to sacrifice at night and therefore appeal to the forces of darkness so feared by the community.

Pliny in Bithynia, however, had tried to find out what it was that Christians actually believed. He recognised the relative harmlessness of their beliefs in themselves. However, Roman authorities did not even approve the institution of a fire brigade when it was necessary because of fears that it would be used as a base for political operations. When a sect was completely out of control, separatist, disdainful of "culture", popular and prophesying mayhem, it was a dreadful threat to civic order. Christianity touched every paranoid nerve of even a "secure" Roman authority. Christians recognised the authority of the Emperor and the State but both came second to the Christ. Thus on both a popular level and that of the State, a religion which denied any right of the gods to protect the State was a cause for fear.

▩ *Christianity in the Third Century* ▩

As the third century progressed, educated Christians grew more confident in representing their religion to intellectuals and philosophers as better than ancestral tradition. Many of these were trained in classical literature and philosophy and knew the best ground from which to convince their opponents. Those who were unconvinced fought back. Even in these intellectual debates, however, there was dialogue, a forum whereby ideas were exchanged. One system had every opportunity to affect the other. Christians became stronger, more numerous, less foreign. Religions looked to Christianity to find a revitalisation of tradition. Admiration for the way Christians clung to their allegiance to Christ and their beliefs in the face of persecution replaced the feeling that they were "weirdos". Much conversion happened because known Christians talked to and convinced the people around them of the value of their religion.

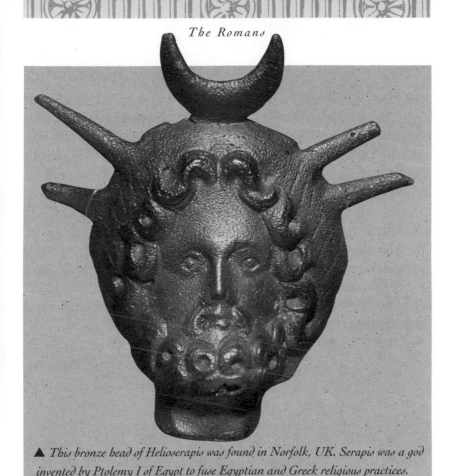

▲ *This bronze head of Helioserapis was found in Norfolk, UK. Serapis was a god invented by Ptolemy I of Egypt to fuse Egyptian and Greek religious practices. Serapis was later joined to Helios, the sun god. Both the face and the rays of light inspired later Christian iconography, though the crescent moon was omitted.*

Society began to accept Christians. However in the fragmenting political world of the third century, anyone who was different, who would not cooperate with the insecure government of the day, was at risk. When the great reconstructor of the Roman world, Diocletian, restored order at the end of that century, he persecuted Christians with particular virulence because religious cohesion was as vital a plank in his program to bring the Roman world together as it had been with Augustus. Yet the religion he promoted was moving inexorably towards monotheism. The major rival to Christianity became Sol Invictus, the unconquered sun, whose birthday feast was celebrated on 25th December.

▣ *The Perplexities of Being Christian* ▣

As Christians became more accepted by people around them, they found life increasingly more complex. Could someone who apostatised, that is sacrificed to the gods to avoid death, be readmitted to the religion after the persecution abated? Should one seek martyrdom? Was it wrong to hide from the authorities? Were the Donatists, a fanatical group in North Africa, the "real" Christians as they believed or, as everyone else thought, a heretical sect? What was the "true" relationship between God the Father and God the Son? Was Christ really God or just the Son of God? If so, how could Christianity have only one god? Could a Christian be a magistrate in the State? If so, how did he deal with the religious ritual attached to his office and the respect which was due to the Emperor? How could he be a soldier?

▣ *Christianity Triumphs* ▣

Christianity finally grew too important to be ignored. The last persecutions were carried out by Diocletian and his fellow emperor Galerius who, according to Christian sources, met a suitably horrible end. After Diocletian's death, the Empire was united under the victor of a civil war, Constantine. He believed he won the decisive Battle of the Milvian Bridge after seeing a sign of the Cross accompanied by the message "By this sign you will conquer". The Christian symbol XP (Chi rho), the first letters of "Christ" in Greek, were painted on his soldiers' shields and they won. The Roman state had a new protector. Yet "Sol Invictus" did not immediately die out. Constantine still favoured this god as well. Christ won, but aspects of the Christ worshipped after the reign of Constantine closely resembled Sol and eventually he shared his birthday.

"Paganism" became the new term of abuse. As Christians became entrenched in the system of the State, those who clung to ancestral

▶ *An early Christian mosaic dating to the 4th or 5th century found in Tunisia in Africa. The inscription would include the person's name and date of death. The equivalent of "Requiescat in Pace" may be partly seen along with the chi rho symbol of Christianity.*

practice were marginalised. Only one emperor after the death of Constantine rejected Christianity. He was known as "Julian the Apostate" and was hated by Christian writers for his belief that Greek philosophy had far more to offer than Christ. The last to desert tradition were the inhabitants of villages, pagani. They still had to deal with the forces of nature on an everyday basis and were unconvinced of the value of Christianity. Roman religion reverted to what it had once been: an attempt by the peasant farmer who eked a living from the soil to propitiate the spirits of his farmland.

Within years of attaining acceptance within the State, Christianity fragmented. West quarrelled with East, "heretics" with mainstream orthodoxy and so on. The Council of Nicaea was organised in 325 to solve disputes. The adjudicator was none other than Constantine himself. The side he favoured became dominant and founded the basis of the power of the Church at Rome. It became a chief legitimator of the Roman State and Roman civilisation.

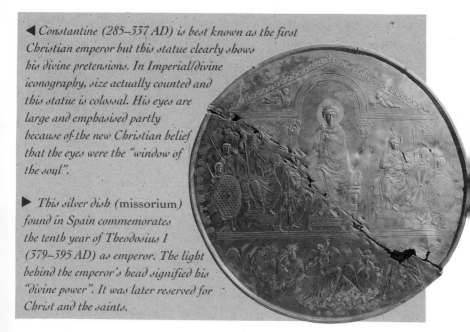

◀ Constantine (285–337 AD) is best known as the first Christian emperor but this statue clearly shows his divine pretensions. In Imperial/divine iconography, size actually counted and this statue is colossal. His eyes are large and emphasised partly because of the new Christian belief that the eyes were the "window of the soul".

▶ This silver dish (missorium) found in Spain commemorates the tenth year of Theodosius I (379–395 AD) as emperor. The light behind the emperor's head signified his "divine power". It was later reserved for Christ and the saints.

The End of Empire

The rise and fall of civilisation captures the human imagination. How can heights achieved in literature, architecture and social organisation change and decay? Why did Rome, an unparalleled success story in the ancient world, fray and crumble? Why was western Europe not able to recapture the science and understanding of the world for a thousand years until the Renaissance? These questions we still ask today were asked in the eighteenth century by the English scholar Edward Gibbon, the most influential writer on "the Fall of Rome", as he sat among the ruins of the Roman forum listening to "barefooted fryars" singing vespers in the temple of Jupiter. How do we explain the end of Rome?

Barbarians at the Gates

The answer that appears self evident is that Roman civilisation fell because the Roman Empire was invaded by barbarians in the late fourth and fifth centuries. In 378 AD Goths defeated a Roman army and slew the Roman emperor Valens at Adrianople, north of modern Istanbul. They roamed freely throughout the Empire and, despite concluding a treaty with the Romans, invaded Italy and sacked Rome in 410. While the actual damage to the city was minimal, the emotional reaction was profound — the hermit Saint Jerome cried from his cave north of Jerusalem: "If Rome perishes, what is safe."

In some sense not much was safe. Elsewhere, Vandals, Sueves and Alans crossed the frozen Rhine in the winter of 406 and wandered throughout the Mediterranean provinces before settling in Africa, Spain and southern Gaul. Burgundians later settled in southern Gaul, and

144

▶ *Diocletian set up a tetrarchy (rule of four) to govern the Empire. The arrangement, here commemorated by a statue, worked while Diocletian was in power but broke down later in the civil wars from which Constantine emerged victor. The tetrarchy and its collapse indicate the problems in size and administration which the Romans suffered in the 3rd century AD.*

Franks, who give their name to France, in northern Gaul. In 476 the last Emperor in the West, Romulus Augustulus, was deposed and pensioned off to a quiet suburban life. The Empire was "barbarian" and the "Dark Ages" had begun.

▦ *Gibbon's View* ▦

Yet while barbarian invasion seemed to explain much, there was still room to speculate. The notion that there was a Roman Empire in 475, but not one in 477, is not always satisfying in its reasoning. Edward Gibbon, a product of Enlightenment rationalism, proposed in *The History of the Decline and Fall of the Roman Empire* that an internal threat, Christianity, sapped the moral fibre of Rome and left it a decayed and ailing beast ready to be picked off by an external threat, barbarian invasion. The moral might of "Roma", the iron resolve of her legions, the innate virtue of her citizenry were eroded by the corrupting influence of Christianity which promoted a mystic and, to Gibbon, useless contemplation of the other world, just at the time barbarians swarmed around her borders. Unable to defend itself any longer, Roman civilisation fell before the onslaught, and the Empire was replaced by a barbaric age of Medieval mysticism.

145

▲ *Justinian (527–565 AD) did a great deal to revive the prestige and power of the Roman Empire in his long reign. This mosaic is in the church of San Vitale in Ravenna. It shows Justinian with the bishop Maximian and their councillors.*

❋ *Why Rome Fell — Some Other Reasons!* ❋

Many other reasons for "Rome's Fall" have been suggested. These range from the possible to the comic, and more often than not, reflect the prejudice of the people who proposed them: abolition of gods, absence of character, anarchy, apathy, bankruptcy, bastardisation, Bolshevisation, bread and circuses, capitalism, celibacy, childlessness, climatic deterioration, communism, complacency, deforestation, degeneration of intellect, degeneration of race, disarmament, earthquakes, economic recession, emancipation of slaves, eradication of the best, female emancipation, gluttony, gout, homosexuality, hypothermia, impotence, inertia, lack of male dignity, lack of army discipline, lack of seriousness, luxury, malaria, orgies, orientalisation, pacifism, poisoning because of lead pipes, prostitution, psychoses, sensuality, servility, sinfulness, stress, taxation and terrorism.

▲ *Accompanying the mosaic of Justinian is an equally beautiful depiction of his wife, Theodora. She was an actress whose intelligence and loyalty were shown at important crises in Justinian's life. She died in 548, possibly soon after the mosaic was made.*

The unifying feature behind these internal explanations is the moral tone, decadence, decay, and decline. And the consistent external explanation that is never far behind these largely moral reasons is the barbarians who spelt the death knell for Roman civilisation and, in some cases, were perceived as moral agents of the Divine Will sent to purify.

Rome and the West

It is part of human nature to interpret change as moral decay, as things becoming worse. In 146 BC at the final destruction of Carthage, its conqueror Scipio Aemilianus wondered how long Rome could maintain its supremacy. He and others wondered whether Rome would quickly become morally debilitated. 550 years later, when barbarians were attacking the city of Trier in northern Gaul, a contemporary author, Salvian, lamented that the population was more interested in watching games in the Amphitheatre than in the crumbling world about them. Yet, if we leave aside moral explanation and concentrate instead on our modern society's debt to ancient Rome, we will understand that, although the city was sacked and the military domination of Rome disappeared, the social context and idea of Rome did not die. A vivid expression of this is Roman Catholicism.

Catholicism developed from a barely tolerated and at times persecuted sect to an official and powerful religion with the conversion of the emperor Constantine in 312. Even as the Empire broke up, Catholicism was, and remained for a thousand years, an expression of "*Romanitas*", the quality of being Roman. The Catholic administrative districts preserved the internal divisions of the late Empire, with some provincial and diocese boundaries in Europe today dating back nearly two thousand years. Catholicism preserved Latin as the language of liturgy and education. "Classical" education continued in the monasteries and cathedral schools of medieval Europe. The basis of that education, classical writers like Cicero, Virgil and Livy, who otherwise would have been lost, were preserved and transmitted. The origin of the modern university system in the twelfth century is found in the structure of the cathedral school and the reintroduction into the syllabus of the philosophy of Aristotle in Latin translation.

Rome's Legacy

Many of the hallmarks of modern society are likewise inherited from the Romans — law and law codes, coinage, taxation, and the modern day "Romance" dialects of Europe are derived from Latin (Spanish, Italian, French, Romanian, Raetish in Switzerland). The concept of the "Senate" as a seat of government in Australia and America, and political ideas such as a republic and liberty have a distinct Roman flavour. Even the Pope is called Pontifex Maximus.

▨ *Byzantium — the Empire in the East* ▨

Constantine, the first Christian emperor, moved his capital to Byzantium, a city which bridged Europe and Asia. He called it "New Rome" giving rise to the division of Empire between East and West in 395. The split between "New Rome" and the old became apparent in the course of the fourth century. The problems that beset the western part of Empire touched only lightly the more compact and urban East. There, Roman civilisation, even Roman political and military structures, continued for another thousand years. It survived the tumult of the Middle Ages, the rise of Islam, and the Latin conquest of the Holy Land during the Crusades, up until its conquest by Turks in 1453. Ironically, Gibbon chose 1453, when the thousand year old walls of Constantine's city crumbled before Turkish artillery and the Crescent replaced the Cross in the ancient church, the Hagia Sophia, as the point to finish his History. The greatest author of Rome's "decline and fall" had traversed the entire Middle Ages in search of a suitable terminus for his work.

▨ *The Fall of Rome — a Complex Process* ▨

The process known as "the Fall of Rome" is therefore more complex than appears at first sight. In military and political terms the Roman Empire did fragment. In the fifth century, the central administration ceased to function, army units were disbanded and "privatised", the city was sacked and the last emperor was deposed in 476. Local custom and forms of government reasserted themselves throughout the Empire, eventually giving rise to the states of Europe. Yet in social terms the qualities of Roman civilisation endured and still live with us today in western society, in government, language, social organisation, art and literature. In that sense Roman civilisation has never left us.

149

Some Important Dates in Roman History

BC

753	Traditional date for the founding of Rome by Romulus and Remus
509	Exile of the last King Tarquinius the Proud and the institution of the Republic
	First secession of the Plebs
264-242	First war against Carthage: Rome gains its first overseas province
218-202	Second war against Carthage. Rome defeats Hannibal and gains control of the Western Mediterranean
180	Rome defeats King Antiochus: gains control of the East
146	Complete destruction of Carthage in Africa and Corinth in Greece
91	Outbreak of the Social War between Rome and her Italian allies
89	First civil war between the Sulla and Marius
81	Dictatorship of Sulla
70-49	Age of Pompey, Cicero and Caesar
49	Second outbreak of civil war. Caesar becomes dictator for the first time
44	Assassination of Caesar
43-30	Third outbreak of civil war
31	Caesar's heir Octavian defeats Mark Antony at the Battle of Actium
28	Octavian is named Augustus. Institution of the "Principate"
19	Death of Virgil, author of *The Aeneid*

150

AD

14	Death of Augustus and the accession of Tiberius
37-41	Reign of Caligula
41-54	Reign of Claudius
54-68	Reign of Nero
69	Year of the Four Emperors. Vespasian emerges as emperor of a new dynasty
69-96	Flavian dynasty (Vespasian, Titus, Domitian)
70	Destruction of the Temple of Jerusalem
79	Eruption of Mt Vesuvius: Pompeii and Herculaneum destroyed
98-117	Reign of Trajan: Tacitus and Pliny write in this period
117-138	Reign of Hadrian
161-169	Reign of Marcus Aurelius
193	Death of Commodus
193-235	Severan dynasty
212	Caracalla pronounces all free-born peoples of the Empire citizens of Rome
293	Diocletian re-establishes order in the Roman state. Institutes the "Tetrarchy", rule of four co-emperors
312	Battle of the Milvian Bridge. Constantine defeated Maxentius
313	Edict of Milan. Christianity allowed to exist legally
324	Constantine reunites the Empire
330	Byzantium consecrated as "New Rome"
379	Theodosius I proclaimed Augustus of the eastern parts of the Empire
438	Theodosius II publishes the Theodosian Code of Roman Law
410	First "sack of Rome" by Alaric the Visigoth
476	Romulus Augustulus deposed as Emperor in the West
534	Justinian's Digest of law published

151

Further Reading

Many ancient sources have been translated into readable prose. The following are just some of the sources for Roman History. Exact reference to Cicero has been omitted. There are many volumes of translations of his letters, speeches and philosophical and oratorical works, all of which are fascinating.

Anon., *Lives of the Later Caesars.* (trans. A. Birley), Penguin Books

Caesar, *The Civil Wars.* (trans. J. Gardner), Penguin Books

Caesar, *The Gallic Wars.* (trans. S.A. Handford), Penguin Books

Cassius Dio, *The Roman History: the reign of Augustus.* (trans I. Scott-Kilvert),, Penguin Books

Juvenal, *The Sixteen Satires.* (trans. P. Green), Penguin Books

Livy, *The Early History of Rome.* (trans. A. de Selincourt), Penguin Books

Lucian, *Satirical Sketches.* (trans. P. Turner), Penguin Books

Martial, *The Epigrams.* (trans J. Michie), Penguin Books

Pliny the Elder, *Natural History: a selection.* (trans. J. F. Healy), Penguin Books

Pliny the Younger, *The Letters of the Younger Pliny.* (trans. B. Radice), Penguin Books

Plutarch, *Makers of Rome.* (trans. I. Scott-Kilvert), Penguin Books

Plutarch, *The Fall of the Roman Republic.* (trans. R. Warner), Penguin Books

Suetonius, *The Twelve Caesars.* (trans R. Graves), Penguin Books

Tacitus, *The Annals of Imperial Rome.* (trans. M. Grant), Penguin Books

Virgil, *The Aeneid.* (trans. D. West Knight), Penguin Books

Roman History is an immense subject. The following is a selection of works which have been particularly useful in writing this text or which are of general interest to the reader who may want to know more.

Boardman, J. (et al), *The Roman World.* (Oxford, New York, Oxford University Press, 1988)

Bradley, K., *Slavery and Rebellion in the Roman World 140 B.C.- 70 B.C.* (London, Batsford, 1989)

D'Arms, J. H., *Romans on the Bay of Naples,* (Cambridge, Harvard University Press, 1970)

Harrison, D., (ed), *Pompeii Revisited: the life and death of a Roman town.* (Sydney, Meditarch, 1994)

Fantham, E. (et al), *Women in the Classical World: image and text.* (London/New York, Oxford University Press, 1994)

Garnsey, P. & Saller, R., *The Roman Empire: economy, society, culture,* (Berkeley: University of Chicago Press, 1987)

Giardina, A. (ed), (trans. Lydia G. Cochrane), *The Romans*, (Chicago, University of Chicago Press, 1993)

Hammond, N.G.L. and Scullard, H.H.(edd), *Oxford Classical Dictionary* (2nd edition), (London, Oxford University Press 1970)

Hopkins, K., *Death and Renewal: sociological studies in Roman History*, (Cambridge, Cambridge University Press, 1983)

Keppie, L., *Understanding Roman Inscriptions*, (London, Batsford 1991)

Lefkowitz, M. and Fant, M., *A Woman's Life in Greece and Rome*, (London, Duckworth, 1982)

Millar, F. (et al), *The Roman Empire and its Neighbours*, (London, Weidenfeld and Nicholson, 1966)

Nicolet, Cl., (trans. P Falla), *The World of the Citizen in Republican Rome*, (Berkeley, University of Chicago Press, 1980)

Olivova, V., *Sport and Games in the Ancient World*, (London, Orbis, 1984)

Shelton, J-A, *As the Romans did: a source book in Roman Social History.* (New York/Oxford, Oxford University Press, 1988)

Stambough, J. E., *The Ancient Roman City*, (Baltimore, Johns Hopkins, 1988)

Veyne, P. (ed), (trans. A. Goldhammer), *A History of Private Life: from Pagan Rome to Byzantium*, (Harvard, Belnap, 1987)

Wiedemann, T., *Greek and Roman Slavery*, (Baltimore, Johns Hopkins, 1981)

Zanker, P., (trans. A Shapiro), *The Power of Images in the Age of Augustus*, (Ann Arbor, Michigan, 1990)

Picture Credits

Index

Acknowledgements

I undertook this project as a specialist in Roman political history of the Late Republic with an active interest in the social and political life of the Roman Empire. I would like to thank the people who helped me cover the length of Roman history from 753 BC to the bitter end — whenever that was. Dr Estelle Lazer's knowledge of the material remains of the Roman World and specifically Pompeii has been invaluable in selecting the illustrations and improving the text in many places. Dr Jonathan Barlow wrote Chapter 12 and informed my ignorance at other vital points in the study of the later period of Roman history. I could not have attempted to write many of the later parts of this book without the knowledge gained from teaching with my colleagues Peter Brennan and Léonie Hayne and I certainly would not have survived the process without the support of my partner James Buckman. I have also enjoyed working with Cynthia Blanche, Deborah Nixon and Jenny Coren from Lansdowne Publishing. To them and all my other colleagues and friends who have helped along the way, my warmest thanks.

The Romans

Copyright © Lansdowne Publishing Pty Ltd

Published by Lansdowne Publishing Pty Ltd
Sydney, Australia

First published 1997
Reprinted 1998
This edition published in 1999 by Bookmart Ltd

Publisher: Deborah Nixon
Production Manager: Sally Stokes
Series Editor: Cynthia Blanche
Designer: Robyn Latimer
Project Co-ordinator: Jennifer Coren
Picture Researcher: Jane Lewis

Set in Garamond on QuarkXpress
Printed in Hong Kong by South China Printing Company

National Library of Australia Cataloguing-in-Publication data
Welch, Kathryn Elizabeth
The Romans.

Bibliography.
Includes index.
ISBN 1 86302 666 5

1. Rome – Civilization. I. Title.

937

Map illustration on page 9 by Dianne Bradley